BEST MANAGEMENT QUOTES

BEST MANAGEMENT QUOTES

Suresh Mohan Semwal

PRABHAT PRAKASHAN

Published by
PRABHAT PRAKASHAN PVT. LTD.
4/19 Asaf Ali Road,
New Delhi-110 002 (INDIA)
e-mail: prabhatbooks@gmail.com

ISBN 978-93-5186-921-4
BEST MANAGEMENT QUOTES
by Suresh Mohan Semwal

Edition
2025

Price
₹ 350.00 (Rupees Three Hundred Fifty only)

Printed at
Yash Printographics, Noida

AUTHOR'S NOTE

An idea can change your life. It is not just a saying but a real life experience for me. One idea that changed my perspective towards work and life is by Mr. Jim Rohn, **"Your market value must be greater than your salary".** Think about it. What kind of freedom and respect a person would get in his/her organization if this quote is practiced? This one idea triggered lot of enabling emotions and changed my work style so much so that I am enjoying my life to the fullest with continuous growth. His another quote, **"Lot of hard working people stop working hard on themselves"** still inspires me to keep working harder on self.

Quotes are valuable. They are knowledge, and wisdom and insight. They offer us the opportunity to learn through others. Quotations are great tools to reinforce and reaffirm what we already understand. Sometimes hearing the words of a famous or successful person is enough to help us accept an idea and put it into action. Experience is the best teacher, no doubts about it but waiting for your own experience to teach you everything can be expensive or very late at times. Human beings have the capability to learn from other's experiences too. This fast paced world has lead to lot of changes in our behavior, temperament and expectations too. Our communication and transportation modes are becoming faster and faster every day. We are living in times where people are asked to **produce more with less.**

We are living in times where people are always short on time. With the advent of Google information is no more a scarce commodity but people are now grappling how to maintain their sanity in this information overload.

Keeping all this mind I came up with this idea of compilation of greatest management thoughts of great people. I am sure these thoughts will trigger lot of positivity and inspiration in our day to day lives. It will work like seeds for our fertile mind.

These thoughts are full of experience, wisdom and insights of great people. I am sure you are going to cherish these thoughts throughout your life. Enjoy reading!

"Pleasant mind is productive mind."

—Suresh Mohan Semwal

CONTENTS

LEADERSHIP

A leader is one who sees more than others see, who sees farther than others see, and who sees before others see.

—Leroy Eimes

❖ ❖ ❖

The task of leadership is not to put greatness into people, but to elicit it, for the greatness is there already.

—John Buchan

❖ ❖ ❖

The best executive is the one who has sense enough to pick good men to do what he wants done, and self-restraint enough to keep from meddling with them while they do it.

—Theodore Roosevelt

❖ ❖ ❖

To lead people, walk beside them....
As for the best leaders, the people do not notice their existence.
The next best, the people honor and praise.
The next, the people fear; and the next, the people hate....
When the best leader's work is done the people say,
"We did it ourselves!"

—Lao-Tsu

❖ ❖ ❖

Do not follow where the path may lead. Go instead where there is no path and leave a trail.

—Harold R. McAlindon

❖ ❖ ❖

If I have seen farther than others, it is because I was standing on the shoulder of giants.

—Isaac Newton

❖ ❖ ❖

I am a man of fixed and unbending principles, the first of which is to be flexible at all times.

—Everett Dirksen

❖ ❖ ❖

Leadership: the art of getting someone else to do something you want done because he wants to do it.

—Dwight D. Eisenhower

❖ ❖ ❖

In times of change, learners inherit the Earth, while the learned find themselves beautifully equipped to deal with a world that no longer exists.

—Eric Hoffer

❖ ❖ ❖

The price of greatness is responsibility.

—Winston Churchill

❖ ❖ ❖

I must follow the people. Am I not their leader?

—Benjamin Disraeli

❖ ❖ ❖

Example is not the main thing in influencing others, it is the only thing.

—Albert Schweitzer

❖ ❖ ❖

Leadership and learning are indispensable to each other.

—John F. Kennedy

❖ ❖ ❖

The final test of a leader is that in other men he leaves behind, the conviction and the will to carry on.

—Walter Lippman

❖ ❖ ❖

If your actions inspire others to dream more, learn more, do more and become more, you are a leader.

—John Quincy Adams

❖ ❖ ❖

I cannot give you the formula for success, but I can give you the formula for failure, which is: Try to please everybody.

—Herbert B. Swope

❖ ❖ ❖

High sentiments always win in the end. The leaders who offer blood, toil, tears and sweat always get more out of their followers than those who offer safety and a good time. When it comes to the pinch, human beings are heroic.

—George Orwell

❖ ❖ ❖

Our chief want is someone who will inspire us to be what we know we could be.

—Ralph Waldo Emerson

❖ ❖ ❖

The very essence of leadership is that you have to have vision. You can't blow an uncertain trumpet.

—Theodore M. Hesburgh

❖ ❖ ❖

I think leadership comes from integrity – that you do whatever you ask others to do. I think there are non-obvious ways to lead. Just by providing a good example as a parent, a friend, a neighbor makes it possible for other people to see better ways to do things. Leadership does not need to be a dramatic, fist in the air and trumpets blaring, activity.

—Scott Berkun

❖ ❖ ❖

The leaders who work most effectively, it seems to me, never say I. And that's not because they have trained themselves not to say I. They don't think I. They think we; they think team. They understand their jobs to be to make the team function. They accept responsibility and don't sidestep it, but we gets the credit.... This is what creates trust, what enables you to get the task done

—Peter Drucker

❖ ❖ ❖

Innovation distinguishes between a leader and a follower.

—Steve Jobs

❖ ❖ ❖

As we look ahead into the next century, leaders will be those who empower others.

—Bill Gates

❖ ❖ ❖

It is impossible to imagine anything which better becomes a ruler than mercy.

—Seneca

❖ ❖ ❖

Never doubt that a small group of thoughtful, concerned citizens can change the world. Indeed, it is the only thing that ever has.

—Margaret Mead

❖ ❖ ❖

Management is efficiency in climbing the ladder of success; leadership determines whether the ladder is leaning against the right wall.

—Stephen R. Covey

❖ ❖ ❖

Authority should be seen as a part of leadership, not as a way around it.

—Michael McKinney

❖ ❖ ❖

He who has great power should use it lightly.

—Seneca

❖ ❖ ❖

How do you know you have won? When the energy is coming the other way and when your people are visibly growing individually and as a group.

—Sir John Harvey-Jones

❖ ❖ ❖

He makes a great mistake...who supposes that authority is firmer or better established when it is founded by force than that which is welded by affection.

—Terence

❖ ❖ ❖

The leader must know, must know that he knows, and must be able to make it abundantly clear to those around him that he knows.

—Clarence Randall

❖ ❖ ❖

You don't lead by pointing and telling people some place to go. You lead by going to that place and making a case.

—Ken Kesey

❖ ❖ ❖

As a leader, you're probably not doing a good job unless your employees can do a good impression of you when you're not around.

—**Patrick Lencioni**

❖ ❖ ❖

Leadership is difficult but it is not complex.

—**Michael McKinney**

❖ ❖ ❖

Look over your shoulder now and then to be sure someone's following you.

—**Henry Gilmer**

❖ ❖ ❖

Leadership is not magnetic personality, that can just as well be a glib tongue. It is not making friends and influencing people, that is flattery. Leadership is lifting a person's vision to higher sights, the raising of a person's performance to a higher standard, the building of a personality beyond its normal limitations.

—**Peter F. Drucker**

❖ ❖ ❖

Leadership is the ability to establish standards and manage a creative climate where people are self-motivated toward the mastery of long-term constructive goals, in a participatory environment of mutual respect, compatible with personal values.

—**Mike Vance**

❖ ❖ ❖

The older I get, the less I listen to what people say and the more I look at what they do.

—**Andrew Carnegie**

❖ ❖ ❖

Leadership is not so much about technique and methods as it is about opening the heart. Leadership is about inspiration—of oneself and of others. Great leadership is about human experiences, not processes. Leadership is not a formula or a program, it is a human activity that comes from the heart and considers the hearts of others. It is an attitude, not a routine.

—Lance Secretan, Industry Week, October 12, 1998

❖ ❖ ❖

More than anything else today, followers believe they are part of a system, a process that lacks heart. If there is one thing a leader can do to connect with followers at a human, or better still a spiritual level, it is to become engaged with them fully, to share experiences and emotions, and to set aside the processes of leadership, we have learned by rote.

—Lance Secretan, Industry Week, October 12, 1998

❖ ❖ ❖

There is no power on earth that can neutralize the influence of a high, simple, and useful life.

—Booker T. Washington

❖ ❖ ❖

He is greatest whose strength carries up the most hearts by the attraction of his own.

—Henry Ward Beecher

❖ ❖ ❖

Max DePree popularized the idea that leadership is an art. So much of what a leader does cannot be objectively measured. To reduce leadership to a set of algorithms is to remove it from its context; to ignore the complexities, the contradictions, and the possibilities. Artists must deal with uncertainty, contradictions and diversity almost by definition. Leaders need to have this capacity.

—Michael McKinney

❖ ❖ ❖

Leadership is getting people to work for you when they are not obligated.

—Fred Smith

❖ ❖ ❖

Into the hands of every individual is given a marvelous power for good or evil—the silent, unconscious, unseen influence of his life. This is simply the constant radiation of what man really is, not what he pretends to be.

—William George Jordan

❖ ❖ ❖

Never doubt that a small group of thoughtful committed citizens can change the world. Indeed, it is the only thing that ever has.

—Margaret Mead

❖ ❖ ❖

My own definition of leadership is this: The capacity and the will to rally men and women to a common purpose and the character which inspires confidence.

—General Montgomery

❖ ❖ ❖

It is no use walking anywhere to preach unless our walking is our preaching.

—St. Francis of Assisi

❖ ❖ ❖

In the course of history, there comes a time when humanity is called to shift to a new level of consciousness, to reach a higher moral ground. A time when we have to shed our fear and give hope to each other. That time is now.

—Wangari Maathai

❖ ❖ ❖

Before you are a leader, success is all about growing

yourself. When you become a leader, success is all about growing others.

—Jack Welch

❖ ❖ ❖

I think that the best training a top manager can be engaged in is management by example. I want to make sure there is no discrepancy between what we say and what we do. If you preach accountability and then promote somebody with bad results, it doesn't work. I personally believe the best training is management by example. Don't believe what I say. Believe what I do.

—Carlos Ghosn, CEO, Renault-Nissan

❖ ❖ ❖

Leadership is a posture and a choice, not a role that must be bestowed on you. Step up and be a leader when no one is watching or expecting you to do so.

—John Izzo and Marshall Goldsmith, Stepping Up

❖ ❖ ❖

When the conduct of men is designed to be influenced, persuasion, kind, unassuming persuasion, should ever be adopted. It is an old and a true maxim, that a drop of honey catches more flies than a gallon of gall.

—Abraham Lincoln February 22, 1842
in Temperance Address

❖ ❖ ❖

I strongly believe that the responsibility of leadership is to shape the debate—to practice and project the right attributes—whether in a business enterprise, in our society, and even in our religions.

—Farooq Kathwari, CEO, Ethan Allen

❖ ❖ ❖

If you don't understand that you work for your mislabeled 'subordinates,' then you know nothing of leadership. You know only tyranny.

—Dee Hock

❖ ❖ ❖

The led must not be compelled; they must be able to choose their own leader.

—Albert Einstein

❖ ❖ ❖

Nearly all men can stand adversity, but if you want to test a man's character, give him power.

—Abraham Lincoln

❖ ❖ ❖

Lead and inspire people. Don't try to manage and manipulate people. Inventories can be managed but people must be lead.

—Ross Perot

❖ ❖ ❖

Those who try to lead the people can only do so by following the mob.

—Oscar Wilde

❖ ❖ ❖

The function of leadership is to produce more leaders, not more followers.

—Ralph Nader

❖ ❖ ❖

No institution can possibly survive if it needs geniuses or supermen to manage it. It must be organized in such a way as to be able to get along under a leadership composed of average human beings.

—Peter Drucker

❖ ❖ ❖

A leader is a dealer in hope.

—Napoleon Bonaparte

❖ ❖ ❖

To be able to lead others, a man must be willing to go forward alone.

—Harry Truman

❖ ❖ ❖

Example is not the main thing in influencing others; it is the only thing.

—Albert Schweitzer

❖ ❖ ❖

People ask the difference between a leader and a boss. The leader works in the open, and the boss in covert.

—Theodore Roosevelt

❖ ❖ ❖

The leader has to be practical and a realist, yet must talk the language of the visionary and the idealist.

—Eric Hoffer

❖ ❖ ❖

Leadership is practiced not so much in words as in attitude and in actions.

—Harold S. Geneen

❖ ❖ ❖

Leaders must be close enough to relate to others, but far enough ahead to motivate them.

—John Maxwell

❖ ❖ ❖

The key to successful leadership today is influence, not authority.

—Kenneth Blanchard

❖ ❖ ❖

Never tell people how to do things. Tell them what to do and they will surprise you with their ingenuity.

—General George Patton

❖ ❖ ❖

Leadership is a potent combination of strategy and character. But if you must be without one, be without the strategy.

—Norman Schwarzkopf

❖ ❖ ❖

The growth and development of people is the highest calling of leadership.

—Harvey S. Firestone

❖ ❖ ❖

One of the tests of leadership is the ability to recognize a problem before it becomes an emergency.

—Arnold Glasow

❖ ❖ ❖

Leaders conceive and articulate goals that lift people out of their petty preoccupations and unite them in pursuit of objectives worthy of their best efforts.

—John Gardner

❖ ❖ ❖

The ability to summon positive emotions during periods of intense stress lies at the heart of effective leadership.

—Jim Loehr

❖ ❖ ❖

People will emulate leaders' behaviors, believing they have silent permission to parrot actions demonstrated at the top of the power hierarchy.

—Phil Buckley

❖ ❖ ❖

Leader in its most important sense means being the agent of your own life, influencing the things you care about most in the world to make it a richer life.

—Stewart Friedman, Total Leadership

❖ ❖ ❖

If you want to build a ship, don't herd people together to collect wood and don't assign them tasks and work, but rather teach them to long for the endless immensity of the sea.

—Antoine de Saint-Exupery

❖ ❖ ❖

The true test of character is not how much we know how to do, but how we behave when we don't know what to do.

—Jon Holt

❖ ❖ ❖

The best leaders are those most interested in surrounding themselves with assistants and associates smarter than they are. They are frank in admitting this and are willing to pay for such talents.

—Amos Parrish

❖ ❖ ❖

The quality of a leader is reflected in the standards they set for themselves.

—Ray Kroc

❖ ❖ ❖

The very essence of leadership is that you have to have a vision.

—Theodore Hesburgh

❖ ❖ ❖

A good leader inspires people to have confidence in the

leader, a great leader inspires people to have confidence in themselves.

—Eleanor Roosevelt

❖ ❖ ❖

Leadership cannot really be taught. It can only be learned.

—Harold Geneen

❖ ❖ ❖

Leadership is the special quality which enables people to stand up and pull the rest of us over the horizon.

—James Fisher

❖ ❖ ❖

Leadership should be more participative than directive, more enabling than performing.

—Mary D. Poole

❖ ❖ ❖

Leadership involves finding a parade and getting in front of it.

—John Naisbitt

❖ ❖ ❖

Leadership is solving problems. The day soldiers stop bringing you their problems is the day you have stopped leading them. They have either lost confidence that you can help or concluded you do not care. Either case is a failure of leadership.

—Colin Powell

❖ ❖ ❖

Leadership should be born out of the understanding of the needs of those who would be affected by it.

—Marian Anderson

❖ ❖ ❖

A sense of humor is part of the art of leadership, of getting along with people, of getting things done.

—Dwight David Eisenhower

❖ ❖ ❖

There is no passion to be found playing small—in settling for a life that is less than the one you are capable of living.

—Nelson Mandela

❖ ❖ ❖

Leadership is the lifting of a man's vision to higher sights, the raising of a man's performance to a higher standard, the building of a man's personality beyond its normal limitations.

—Peter Drucker

❖ ❖ ❖

Leaders are designers, stewards, and teachers. They are responsible for building organisations where people continually expand their abilities to understanding complexity, clarify vision, and improve shared mental models—that is, they are responsible for learning.

—Peter Senge, The Fifth Discipline

❖ ❖ ❖

Presidents, leaders, to be effective have to represent the whole to the parts and to the world outside. They may live in the centre but they must not be the centre. To reinforce the common sense they must be a constant teacher, ever travelling, ever talking, ever listening, the chief missionary of the common cause.

—Charles Handy

❖ ❖ ❖

The best leaders are the best notetakers, best askers and best learners.

—Tom Peters

❖ ❖ ❖

MANAGEMENT

Start with the end in mind.

— Stephen R. Covey

❖ ❖ ❖

Management must manage!

—Harold S. Geneen

❖ ❖ ❖

All time management begins with planning.

—Tom Greening

❖ ❖ ❖

Lots of folks confuse bad management with destiny.

—Kin Hubbard

❖ ❖ ❖

The smaller the function, the greater the management.

—C. Northcote Parkinson

❖ ❖ ❖

Eliminate numerical quotas, including Management by Objectives.

—W. Edwards Deming

❖ ❖ ❖

Management is doing things right; leadership is doing the right things.

—Peter F. Drucker

❖ ❖ ❖

No business in the world has ever made more money with poorer management.

—Bill Terry

❖ ❖ ❖

If an artist can manage his career, well, that is half the battle to becoming successful.

—Martin Dansky

❖ ❖ ❖

Management by objective works—if you know the objectives. Ninety percent of the time you don't.

—Peter F. Drucker

❖ ❖ ❖

Reduce the layers of management. They put distance between the top of an organization and the customers.

—Donald Rumsfeld

❖ ❖ ❖

Effective leadership is putting first things first. Effective management is discipline, carrying it out.

—Stephen R. Covey

❖ ❖ ❖

Effective leadership is not about making speeches or being liked; leadership is defined by results not attributes.

—Peter F. Drucker

❖ ❖ ❖

Instead of forming new words I recommend to you any kind of artful management by which you may be able to give cost to old ones.

—Horace

❖ ❖ ❖

Democracy is a form of government in which it is permitted to wonder aloud what the country could do under first-class management.

—Doug Larson

❖ ❖ ❖

If you're playing baseball and thinking about managing, you're crazy. You'd be better off thinking about being an owner.

—Casey Stengel

❖ ❖ ❖

The conventional definition of management is getting work done through people, but real management is developing people through work.

—Agha Hasan Abedi

❖ ❖ ❖

Good management is the art of making problems so interesting and their solutions so constructive that everyone wants to get to work and deal with them.

—Paul Hawken

❖ ❖ ❖

I don't think a manager should be judged by whether he wins the pennant, but by whether he gets the most out of the twenty-five men he's been given.

—Chuck Tanner

❖ ❖ ❖

When a management team with a reputation for brilliance tackles a business with a reputation for bad economics, it is the reputation of the business that remains intact.

—Warren Buffett

❖ ❖ ❖

Management means, in the last analysis, the substitution of thought for brawn and muscle, of knowledge for folklore and superstition, and of cooperation for force.

—Peter F. Drucker

❖ ❖ ❖

Most people do not receive nearly enough appreciation. How can this be when appreciation is free, easy, and readily available? All you have to do is speak. Go give some away now.

—Rhoberta Shaler

❖ ❖ ❖

In the modern world of business, it is useless to be a creative original thinker unless you can also sell what you create. Management cannot be expected to recognize a good idea unless it is presented to them by a good salesman.

—David Ogilvy

❖ ❖ ❖

Organization doesn't really accomplish anything. Plans don't accomplish anything, either. Theories of management don't much matter. Endeavors succeed or fail because of the people involved. Only by attracting the best people will you accomplish great deeds.

—Colin Powell

❖ ❖ ❖

Determine that the thing can and shall be done, and then we shall find the way.

—Abraham Lincoln

❖ ❖ ❖

The quality of a man's life is in direct proportion to his commitment to excellence, regardless of his chosen field of endeavor.

—Vince Lombardi

❖ ❖ ❖

One rule of action more important than all others is consists in never doing anything that someone else can do for you.

—Calvin Coolidge

❖ ❖ ❖

Take time to deliberate, but when the time for action has arrived, stop thinking and go in.

—Napoleon Bonaparte

❖ ❖ ❖

Always mistrust a subordinate who never finds fault with his superior.

—John Churton Collins

❖ ❖ ❖

Never give an order that can't be obeyed.

—General Douglas MacAuthur

❖ ❖ ❖

Reason and judgment are the qualities of a leader.

—Tacitus

❖ ❖ ❖

An army of lions commanded by a deer will never be an army of lions.

—Napoleon Bonaparte

❖ ❖ ❖

The measure of a man is what he does with power.

—Greek Proverb

❖ ❖ ❖

If you command wisely, you'll be obeyed cheerfully.

—Thomas Fuller

❖ ❖ ❖

Vivacity, leadership, must be had, and we are not allowed to be nice in choosing. We must fetch the pump with dirty water, if clean cannot be had.

—Ralph Waldo Emerson

❖ ❖ ❖

One should never forbid what one lacks the power to prevent.

—Napoleon Bonaparte

❖ ❖ ❖

Go before the people with your example, and be laborious in their affairs.

—Confucius

❖ ❖ ❖

The art of choosing men is not nearly so difficult as the art of enabling those one has chosen to attain their full worth.

—**Napoleon Bonaparte**

❖ ❖ ❖

We're all working together; that's the secret.

—**Sam Walton**

❖ ❖ ❖

Appreciate everything your associates do for the business. If people believe in themselves, it's amazing what they can accomplish.

—**Sam Walton**

❖ ❖ ❖

The people who are doing the work are the moving force behind the Macintosh. My job is to create a space for them, to clear out the rest of the organization and keep it at bay.

—**Steve Jobs**

❖ ❖ ❖

Team, it turned out that Michael Dell wasn't perfect at predicting the future. Based on today's stock market close, Apple is worth more than Dell. Stocks go up and down and things may be different tomorrow but I thought it was worth a moment of reflection today.

—**Steve Jobs**

❖ ❖ ❖

If I attack alone, I might turn out to be a wimp. But with a strong business team behind me, I am a force to contend with.

—**Ajaero Tony Martins**

❖ ❖ ❖

Go to the wolf, consider its ways and be wise. A wolf will never hunt alone; it hunts in packs because it knows the power of team work.

—**Ajaero Tony Martins**

❖ ❖ ❖

Talent wins games, but teamwork and intelligence wins championships.

—**Michael Jordan**

❖ ❖ ❖

Strength lies in differences, not in similarities.

—**Stephen Covey**

❖ ❖ ❖

Individual commitment to a group effort—that is what makes a team work.

—**Vincent Lombardi**

❖ ❖ ❖

Teamwork is the ability to work together toward a common vision. It is the fuel that allows common people to attain uncommon results.

—**Andrew Carnegie**

❖ ❖ ❖

No man will make a great leader who wants to do it all himself, or to get all the credit for doing it.

—**Andrew Carnegie**

❖ ❖ ❖

It is amazing what can be accomplished when nobody cares about who gets the credit.

—**Robert Yates**

❖ ❖ ❖

There's nothing greater in the world than when somebody on the team does something good, and everybody gathers around to pat him on the back.

—**Billy Martin**

❖ ❖ ❖

One man can be a crucial ingredient on a team, but one man cannot make a team.

—**Kareem Abdul-Jabbar**

❖ ❖ ❖

The way a team plays as a whole determines its success. You may have the greatest bunch of individual stars in the world, but if they don't play together, the club won't be worth a dime.

—Babe Ruth

❖ ❖ ❖

A single arrow is easily broken, but not ten in a bundle.

—Japanese proverb

❖ ❖ ❖

It is amazing how much people get done if they do not worry about who gets the credit.

—Swahili proverb

❖ ❖ ❖

A team is more than a collection of people. It is a process of give and take.

—Barbara Glacel and Emile Robert Jr.

❖ ❖ ❖

Interdependent people combine their own efforts with the efforts of others to achieve their greatest success.

—Stephen Covey

❖ ❖ ❖

The ratio of Wes to Is is the best indicator of the development of a team.

—Lewis B. Ergen

❖ ❖ ❖

The leaders who work most effectively, it seems to me, never say 'I.' And that's not because they have trained themselves not to say 'I.' They don't think 'I.' They think 'we'; they think 'team.' They understand their job to be to make the team function. They accept responsibility and don't sidestep it, but 'we' gets the credit.... This is what creates trust, what enables you to get the task done.

—Peter Drucker

❖ ❖ ❖

Coming together is a beginning. Keeping together is progress. Working together is success.

—Henry Ford

❖ ❖ ❖

Teamwork is the fuel that allows common people to attain uncommon results.

—Anonymous

❖ ❖ ❖

Teams share the burden and divide the grief.

—Doug Smith

❖ ❖ ❖

Individual commitment to a group effort—that is what makes a team work a company work, a society work, a civilization work.

—Vince Lombardi

❖ ❖ ❖

Build for your team a feeling of oneness, of dependence on one another and of strength to be derived by unity.

—Vince Lombardi

❖ ❖ ❖

In teamwork, silence isn't golden, it's deadly.

—Mark Sanborn

❖ ❖ ❖

A group becomes a team when each member is sure enough of himself and his contribution to praise the skill of the others.

—Norman S. Hidle

❖ ❖ ❖

The greatest danger a team faces isn't that it won't become successful, but that it will, and then cease to improve.

—Mark Sanborn

❖ ❖ ❖

What we need to do is learn to work in the system, by which I mean that everybody, every team, every platform, every division, every component is there not for individual competitive profit or recognition, but for contribution to the system as a whole on a win-win basis.

—W. Edward Deming

❖ ❖ ❖

It's easy to get good players. Getting them to play together, that's the hard part.

—Casey Stengel

❖ ❖ ❖

Teamwork is so important that it is virtually impossible for you to reach the heights of your capabilities or make the money that you want without becoming very good at it.

—Brian Tracy

❖ ❖ ❖

The basic building block of good teambuilding is for a leader to promote the feeling that every human being is unique and adds value.

—Anonymous

❖ ❖ ❖

No matter what accomplishments you make, somebody helped you.

—Althea Gibson

❖ ❖ ❖

Team player: Once who unites others toward a shared destiny through sharing information and ideas, empowering others and developing trust.

—Dennis Kinlaw

❖ ❖ ❖

Light is the task where many share the toil.

—Homer

❖ ❖ ❖

No member of a crew is praised for the rugged individuality of his rowing.

—Ralph Waldo Emerson

❖ ❖ ❖

A major reason capable people fail to advance is that they don't work well with their colleagues.

—Lee Iacocca

❖ ❖ ❖

T.E.A.M. = Together everyone achieves more.

—Anonymous

❖ ❖ ❖

If you pick the right people and give them the opportunity to spread their wings—and put compensation as a carrier behind it—you almost don't have to manage them.

—Jack Welch

❖ ❖ ❖

Make your top managers rich and they will make you rich.

—Robert H. Johnson

❖ ❖ ❖

Catch someone doing something right.

—Kenneth Blanchard and Spencer Johnson

❖ ❖ ❖

Never try to teach a pig to sing; it wastes your time and it annoys the pig.

—Paul Dickson

❖ ❖ ❖

Surround yourself with the best people you can find, delegate authority, and don't interfere as long as the policy you've decided upon is being carried out.

—Ronald Reagan

❖ ❖ ❖

Always recognize that human individuals are ends, and do not use them as means to your end.

—Immanuel Kant

❖ ❖ ❖

People are definitely a company's greatest asset. It doesn't make any difference whether the product is cars or cosmetics. A company is only as good as the people it keeps.

—Mary Kay Ash

❖ ❖ ❖

Smart people instinctively understand the dangers of entrusting our future to self-serving leaders who use our institutions—whether in the corporate or social sectors—to advance their own interests.

—Jim Collins

❖ ❖ ❖

A good manager is a man who isn't worried about his own career but rather the careers of those who work for him.

—H.S.M. Burns

❖ ❖ ❖

Withhold not good from them to whom it is due, when it is in the power of thine hand to do it.

—Proverbs

❖ ❖ ❖

TIME MANAGEMENT

A great many people think they are thinking when they are merely rearranging their prejudices.

—William James

❖ ❖ ❖

A man must be master of his hours and days, not their servant.

—William Frederick Book

❖ ❖ ❖

A man who dares to waste one hour of life has not discovered the value of life.

—Charles Darwin

❖ ❖ ❖

A wise person does at once, what a fool does at last. Both do the same thing; only at different times.

—Baltasar Gracian

❖ ❖ ❖

All great achievements require time.

—Maya Angelou

❖ ❖ ❖

All the forces in the world are not so powerful as an idea whose time has come.

—Victor Hugo

❖ ❖ ❖

Anything that is wasted effort represents wasted time. The best management of our time thus becomes linked inseparably with the best utilization of our efforts.

—Ted W. Engstrom

❖ ❖ ❖

Be happy. It's one way of being wise.

—Colette

❖ ❖ ❖

Believe that time is going to help you do what you want.

—William Morris Hunt

❖ ❖ ❖

By the time we've made it, we've had it.

—Malcolm Forbes

❖ ❖ ❖

Clock watchers never seem to be having a good time.

—James Cash Penney

❖ ❖ ❖

Defer no time, delays have dangerous ends.

—William Shakespeare

❖ ❖ ❖

Determine never to be idle. No person will have occasion to complain of the want of time who never loses any. It is wonderful how much can be done if we are always doing.

—Thomas Jefferson

❖ ❖ ❖

Do not dwell in the past, do not dream of the future, concentrate the mind on the present moment.

—Buddha

❖ ❖ ❖

Do not wait; the time will never be just right. Start where you stand, and work with whatever tools you may have at your command, and better tools will be found as you go along.

—Napoleon Hill

❖ ❖ ❖

Don't be fooled by the calendar. There are only as many days in the year as you make use of. One man gets only a week's value out of a year while another man gets a full year's value out of a week.

—Charles Richards

❖ ❖ ❖

Don't watch the clock; do what it does. Keep going.

—Samuel Levenson

❖ ❖ ❖

Don't be afraid to be amazing.

—Andy Offutt Irwin

❖ ❖ ❖

Don't wait. The time will never be just right.

—Napoleon Hill

❖ ❖ ❖

Dost thou love life? Then do not squander time, for that is the stuff life is made of.

—Benjamin Franklin

❖ ❖ ❖

For behold, the kingdom of God is within you.

—Luke 17

❖ ❖ ❖

For time and the world, do not stand still. Change is the law of life. And those who look only to the past or the present are certain to miss the future.

—John F. Kennedy

❖ ❖ ❖

Half of our lives is spent trying to find something to do with the time we have rushed through life trying to save.

—Will Rogers

❖ ❖ ❖

He that rises late must trot all day.

—Benjamin Franklin

❖ ❖ ❖

He that will not sail' til all dangers are over must never put out to sea.

—Thomas Fuller

❖ ❖ ❖

He who know most grieves most for wasted time.

—Dante

❖ ❖ ❖

Heaven is right where you are standing, and that is the place to practice.

—Morehei Ueshiba

❖ ❖ ❖

I don't think of the past. The only thing that matters is the everlasting present.

—W. Somerset Maugham

❖ ❖ ❖

I never hit a shot, not even in practice, without having a very sharp, in-focus picture of it in my head.

—Jack Nicklaus

❖ ❖ ❖

I saw a bank that said 24 Hour Banking, but I don't have that much time.

—Steven Wright

❖ ❖ ❖

I shall not waste my days in trying to prolong them. I shall use my time.

—Ian Fleming

❖ ❖ ❖

If nature puts a burden on a man by making him different, it also gives him a power.

—John Lame Deer

❖ ❖ ❖

If you don't know how you feel, you won't know what you want.

—Barbra Scher

❖ ❖ ❖

If you have time to whine and complain about something then you have the time to do something about it.

—Anthony J. D'Angelo

❖ ❖ ❖

If you haven't got the time to do it right, when will you find the time to do it over?

—Jeffery J. Mayer

❖ ❖ ❖

If you spend too much time thinking about a thing, you'll never get it done.

—Bruce Lee

❖ ❖ ❖

In order for your dreams to come true, you've got to stay awake.

—Charles Durning

❖ ❖ ❖

In the real world, nothing happens at the right place at the right time. It is the job of journalists and historians to correct that.

—Mark Twain

❖ ❖ ❖

It has been my observation that most people get ahead during the time that others waste.

—Henry Ford

❖ ❖ ❖

It is a mistake to look too far ahead. Only one link of the chain of destiny can be handled at a time.

—Winston Churchill

❖ ❖ ❖

It's how we spend our time here and now, that really matters. If you are fed up with the way you have come to interact with time, change it.

—Marcia Wieder

❖ ❖ ❖

It's not the daily increase but daily decrease. Hack away at the unessential.

—Bruce Lee

❖ ❖ ❖

It's not what you are that holds you back, it's what you think you're not.

—Anonymous

❖ ❖ ❖

Joy is an experience, not an attitude.

—Anonymous

❖ ❖ ❖

Learn how to say no. Don't let your mouth overload your back.

—Jim Rohn

❖ ❖ ❖

Lost wealth may be replaced by industry, lost knowledge by study, lost health by temperance or medicine, but lost time is gone forever.

—Samuel Smiles

❖ ❖ ❖

Make measurable progress in reasonable time.

—Jim Rohn

❖ ❖ ❖

Make use of time, let not advantage slip.

—William Shakespeare

❖ ❖ ❖

Many people take no care of their money till they come nearly to the end of it, and others do just the same with their time.

—Johann Wolfgang von Goethe

❖ ❖ ❖

May you live all the days of your life.

—Jonathan Swift

❖ ❖ ❖

Most time is wasted, not in hours, but in minutes. A bucket with a small hole in the bottom gets just as empty as a bucket that is deliberately kicked over.

—Paul J. Meyer

❖ ❖ ❖

Never leave 'till tomorrow which you can do today.

—Benjamin Franklin

❖ ❖ ❖

Never let yesterday use up today.

—Richard H. Nelson

❖ ❖ ❖

No matter what you have done to this moment, you get 24 brand-new hours to spend every single day.

—Brian Tracy

❖ ❖ ❖

Nothing much happens without a dream. For something really great to happen, it takes a really great dream.

—Robert Greenleaf

❖ ❖ ❖

Once you have mastered time, you will understand how true it is that most people overestimate what they can accomplish in a year—and underestimate what they can achieve in a decade!

—Anthony Robbins

❖ ❖ ❖

One always has time enough, if one will apply it well.

—Johann Wolfgang von Goethe

❖ ❖ ❖

One realizes the full importance of time only when there is little of it left. Every man's greatest capital asset is his unexpired years of productive life.

—P.W. Litchfield

❖ ❖ ❖

One worthwhile task carried to a successful conclusion is worth half-a-hundred half-finished tasks.

—Malcolm S. Forbes

❖ ❖ ❖

Ordinary people think merely of spending time. Great people think of using it.

—Anonymous

❖ ❖ ❖

People are always good company when they are doing what they really enjoy.

—Samuel Butler

❖ ❖ ❖

People who never have any time on their hands are those who do the least.

—George C. Lichtenberg

❖ ❖ ❖

Realize that now, in this moment of time, you are creating. You are creating your next moment. That is what's real.

—Sara Paddison

❖ ❖ ❖

Review our priorities, ask the question: What's the best use of our time right now?

—Alan Lakein

❖ ❖ ❖

Set priorities for your goals. A major part of successful living lies in the ability to put first things first. Indeed, the reason most major goals are not achieved is that we spend our time doing second things first.

—Robert J. Mckain

❖ ❖ ❖

So much of our time is spent in preparation, so much in routine, and so much in retrospect, that the amount of each person's genius is confined to a very few hours.

—Ralph Waldo Emerson

❖ ❖ ❖

Something will master and something will serve. Either you run the day or the day runs you; either you run the business or the business runs you.

—Jim Rohn

❖ ❖ ❖

Success in the majority of circumstances depends on knowing how long it takes to succeed.

—Charles De Montesquiu

❖ ❖ ❖

Success is simple. Do what's right, the right way, at the right time.

—Arnold H. Glasgow

❖ ❖ ❖

Take care of the minutes and the hours will take care of themselves.

—Lord Chesterfield

❖ ❖ ❖

The bad news is time flies. The good news is you're the pilot.

—Michael Altshuler

❖ ❖ ❖

The common man is not concerned about the passage of time, the man of talent is driven by it.

—Arthur Shoppenhauer

❖ ❖ ❖

The first hour of the morning is the rudder of the day.

—Henry Ward Beecher

❖ ❖ ❖

The great dividing line between success and failure can be expressed in five words: I did not have time.

—Franklin Field

❖ ❖ ❖

The greatest poverty in America today is time poverty. People have money, but they don't have time.

—Brian Tracy

❖ ❖ ❖

The happiest people spend much time in a state of flow—the state in which people are so involved in an activity that nothing else seems to matter; the experience itself is so enjoyable that people will do it even at great cost, for the sheer sake of doing it.

—Mihaly Csikszentmihalyi

❖ ❖ ❖

The key is in not spending time, but in investing it.

—Stephen R. Covey

❖ ❖ ❖

The less one has to do, the less time one finds to do it in.

—Lord Chesterfield

❖ ❖ ❖

The next time you find yourself in an argument, rather than

defend your position, see if you can see the other point of view first.

—Richard Carlson

❖ ❖ ❖

The only reason for time is so that everything doesn't happen at once.

—Albert Einstein

❖ ❖ ❖

The soul never thinks without a mental picture. **—Aristotle**
The time for action is now. It's never too late to do something.

—Carl Sandburg

❖ ❖ ❖

The time to relax is when you don't have time for it.

—Sydney J. Harris

❖ ❖ ❖

The time you enjoy wasting is not wasted time.

—Bertrand Russell

❖ ❖ ❖

The whole purpose of time management is to enable you to have more time to spend with the people you love, doing the things you enjoy.

—Brian Tracy

❖ ❖ ❖

There's never enough time to do it right, but there's always enough time to do it over.

—Jack Bergman

❖ ❖ ❖

This time, like all times, is a very good one, if we but know what to do with it.

—Ralph Waldo Emerson

❖ ❖ ❖

Those who dream by day are cognizant of many things which escape those who dream only by night.

—Edgar Allan Poe

❖ ❖ ❖

Time = life; therefore, waste your time and waste of your life, or master your time and master your life.

—Alan Lakein

❖ ❖ ❖

Time and the hour run through the roughest day.

—William Shakespeare

❖ ❖ ❖

Time flies. It's up to you to be the navigator.

—Robert Orben

❖ ❖ ❖

Time has no conscience...it doesn't judge...it only mirrors... what you have put into your time...it mirrors back as your life.

—Doug Firebaugh

❖ ❖ ❖

Time has no favorites...and it doesn't become kinder to one over another...it just gives us back...what we put into it....

—Doug Firebaugh

❖ ❖ ❖

Time is a great healer, but a poor beautician.

—Lucille S. Harper

❖ ❖ ❖

Time is amazing...you spend it, and it multiplies...you invest it, and it intensifies...and you ignore it...it passes you by....

—Doug Firebaugh

❖ ❖ ❖

Time is free, but it's priceless. You can't own it, but you can use it. You can't keep it, but you can spend it. Once you've lost it, you can never get it back.

—Harvey Mackay

❖ ❖ ❖

Time is inelastic and inflexible. Time is indispensable. No achievement is possible without time.

—Brian Tracy

❖ ❖ ❖

Time is like money, the less we have of it to spare the further we make it go.

—Josh Billings ❖ ❖ ❖

Time is our most valuable asset, yet we tend to waste it, kill it, and spend it rather than invest it.

—Jim Rohn

❖ ❖ ❖

Time is that which a man is always trying to kill, but which ends in killing him.

—Herbert Spencer

❖ ❖ ❖

Time is the fairest and toughest judge.

—Edgar Quinet

❖ ❖ ❖

Time is the most precious element of human existence. The successful person knows how to put energy into time and how to draw success from time.

—Denis Waitley

❖ ❖ ❖

Time is the scarcest resource of the manager. If it is not managed, nothing else can be managed.

—Peter F. Drucker

❖ ❖ ❖

Time is what we want the most, but what we use worst.

—William Penn

❖ ❖ ❖

Time stays, we go.

—H.L. Mencken

❖ ❖ ❖

Time will explain it all. He is a talker, and needs no questioning before he speaks.

—Euripides

❖ ❖ ❖

Time will take your money, but money won't buy time.

—James Taylor

❖ ❖ ❖

Time, whose tooth gnaws away at everything else, is powerless against truth.

—Thomas Huxley

❖ ❖ ❖

To invent, you need a good imagination and a pile of junk.

—Thomas Edison

❖ ❖ ❖

Try not to have a good time...this is supposed to be educational.

—Charles M. Schulz

❖ ❖ ❖

Until you value yourself, you will not value your time. Until you value your time, you will not do anything with it.

—M. Scott Peck

❖ ❖ ❖

We are most truly ourselves when we achieve the seriousness of a child at play.

—Heroclitus

❖ ❖ ❖

We can no more afford to spend major time on minor things than we can to spend minor time on major things.

—Jim Rohn

❖ ❖ ❖

We must be willing to get rid of the life we've planned, so as to have the life that is waiting for us.

—Joseph Campbell

❖ ❖ ❖

Well-arranged time is the surest mark of a well-arranged mind.

—Pitman

❖ ❖ ❖

What do you want to get done? In what order of importance? Over what period of time? What is the time available? What is the best strategy for application of time to projects for the most effective results?

—Ted W. Engstrom

❖ ❖ ❖

What if, along with our 'to do' list, we had a 'to be' list too?

—Ken Johnston

❖ ❖ ❖

When I am getting ready to reason with a man, I spend one-third of my time thinking about myself and what I am going to say and two-thirds about him and what he is going to say.

—Abraham Lincoln

❖ ❖ ❖

Wherever you are is the entry point.

—Kabir

❖ ❖ ❖

Whether it's the best of times or the worst of times, it's the only time we've got.

—Art Buchwald

❖ ❖ ❖

You cannot do a kindness too soon, for you never know how soon it will be too late.

—Ralph Waldo Emerson

❖ ❖ ❖

You cannot increase the quality or quantity of your achievement or performance except to the degree of which you increase your ability to use your time effectively.

—Brian Tracy

❖ ❖ ❖

You may delay, but time will not.

—Benjamin Franklin

❖ ❖ ❖

You must never find time for anything. If you want time, you must make it

—Charles Buxton

❖ ❖ ❖

GROWTH

A feeling of continuous growth is a wonderful source of motivation and self-confidence.

—Brian Tracy

❖ ❖ ❖

A man who finds no satisfaction in himself will seek for it in vain elsewhere.

—La Rochefoucauld

❖ ❖ ❖

All growth depends upon activity. There is no development physically or intellectually without effort, and effort means work.

—Calvin Coolidge

❖ ❖ ❖

As long as we place millions of Indians at the canter of our thought process, as long as we think of their welfare, their future, their opportunities for self-realization we are on the right track. For India can grow, prosper, flourish only if they grow, prosper, flourish. We cannot grow by any esoteric strategies. Our purchasing power, our economic strength, our marketplace all depends on the prosperity of our people.

—Mukesh Ambani

❖ ❖ ❖

As the sculptor devotes himself to wood and stone, I would devote myself to my soul.

—Toyohiko Kagawa

❖ ❖ ❖

Be not afraid of growing slowly; be afraid only of standing still.

—Chinese Proverb

❖ ❖ ❖

Change and growth take place when a person has risked himself and dares to become involved with experimenting with his own life.

—Herbert Otto

❖ ❖ ❖

China has really succeeded because of its stability. So my feeling is, how are they going to maintain this fantastic stability in a very fast changing economic situation. I think this is a challenge we face, how the global region will evolve in stability with such a fast growth. If they succeed to do that, no doubt, in the next generation it will be the major area of the world, economically.

—Bernard Arnault

❖ ❖ ❖

Climb mountains to see lowlands.

—Chinese Proverb

❖ ❖ ❖

Collect as precious pearls, the words of the wise and virtuous.

—Abd-el-Kadar

❖ ❖ ❖

Conformity is the jailer of freedom and the enemy of growth.

—John F. Kennedy

❖ ❖ ❖

Do not think of your faults, still less of other's faults; look for what is good and strong and try to imitate it. Your faults will drop off, like dead leaves, when their time comes.

—John Ruskin

❖ ❖ ❖

Every day do something that will inch you closer to a better tomorrow.

—Doug Firebaugh

❖ ❖ ❖

Everybody wants to be somebody; nobody wants to grow.

—Johann Wolfgang von Goethe

❖ ❖ ❖

Exert your talents, and distinguish yourself, and don't think of retiring from the world, until the world will be sorry that you retire.

—Samuel Johnson

❖ ❖ ❖

Fear less, hope more, eat less, chew more, whine less, breathe more, talk less, say more, hate less, love more, and good things will be yours.

—Swedish Proverb

❖ ❖ ❖

Follow your honest convictions, and stay strong.

—William Thackeray

❖ ❖ ❖

God ever works with those who work with will.

—Eschylus

❖ ❖ ❖

Growth for the sake of growth is the ideology of the cancer cell.

—Edward Abbey

❖ ❖ ❖

Growth itself contains the germ of happiness.

—Pearl S. Buck

❖ ❖ ❖

He that will not reflect is a ruined man.

—Asian Proverb

❖ ❖ ❖

He who conquers others is strong; He who conquers himself is mighty.

—Lao Tzu

❖ ❖ ❖

Heaven never helps the man who will not act.

—Sophocles

❖ ❖ ❖

Heed the still small voice that so seldom leads us wrong, and never into folly.

—Marquise du Deffand

❖ ❖ ❖

I really want people to know that I've worked hard, very hard, to get to where I am today. This didn't just happen overnight. I started in business over 25 years ago and have found a way to build on what I've learned through every partnership and opportunity.

—Magic Johnson

❖ ❖ ❖

I think that our fundamental belief is that for us growth is a way of life and we have to grow at all times.

—Mukesh Ambani

❖ ❖ ❖

If we all did the things we are capable of, we would astound ourselves.

—Thomas Edison

❖ ❖ ❖

If we are going to carry on growing, and we will, because no country is going to forfeit its right to economic growth, we have to find a way of doing it sustainably.

—Tony Blair

❖ ❖ ❖

If we do not plant knowledge when young, it will give us no shade when we are old.

—Lord Chesterfield

❖ ❖ ❖

If we don't change, we don't grow. If we don't grow, we aren't really living.

—Anatole France

❖ ❖ ❖

If you have an hour, will you not improve that hour, instead of idling it away?

—Lord Chesterfield

❖ ❖ ❖

I'm a big believer in growth. Life is not about achievement, it's about learning and growth, and developing qualities like compassion, patience, perseverance, love, and joy, and so forth. And so if that is the case, then I think our goals should include something which stretches us.

—Jack Canfield

❖ ❖ ❖

In learning to know other things, and other minds, we become more intimately acquainted with ourselves, and are to ourselves better worth knowing.

—Philip Gilbert Hamilton

❖ ❖ ❖

In the end, it is the person you become, not the things you have achieved, that is the most important.

—Les Brown

❖ ❖ ❖

Insist on yourself. Never imitate.

—Ralph Waldo Emerson

❖ ❖ ❖

It is not easy to find happiness in ourselves, and it is not possible to find it elsewhere.

—Agnes Repplier

❖ ❖ ❖

It is only the very wisest and the very stupidest who cannot change.

—Confucius

❖ ❖ ❖

It was our duty to expand. Those who cannot or will not join us are to be pitied. What we want to do, we can do and will do, together. A glorious future!

—Ingvar Kamprad

❖ ❖ ❖

It's tough to say, exactly, what things will look like in three to five years, but there's a lot of work to do in just moving along the path that we've already set out.

—Mark Zuckerberg

❖ ❖ ❖

It's where we go, and what we do when we get there, that tells us who we are.

—Joyce Carol Oates

❖ ❖ ❖

Know thyself means this, that you get acquainted with what you know, and what you can do.

—Menander

❖ ❖ ❖

Knowing yourself is the beginning of all wisdom.

—Aristotle

❖ ❖ ❖

Learn from yesterday, live for today, hope for tomorrow.

—Albert Einstein

❖ ❖ ❖

Learn how to separate the majors and the minors. A lot of people don't do well simply because they major in minor things.

—Jim Rohn

❖ ❖ ❖

Learning how to learn is life's most important skill.

—Anonymous

❖ ❖ ❖

Life is a succession of lessons which must be lived to be understood.

—Ralph Waldo Emerson

❖ ❖ ❖

Life is not about waiting for the storm to pass. It's about learning how to dance in the rain.

—Anonymous

❖ ❖ ❖

Make it thy business to know thyself, which is the most difficult lesson in the world.

—Miguel de Cervantes

❖ ❖ ❖

Men see the faults of others learn a few their virtues, too, find out; But is there one—I have a doubt—Who can his own defects discern?

—Sanskrit Proverb

❖ ❖ ❖

Move fast and break things. Unless you are breaking stuff, you are not moving fast enough.

—Mark Zuckerberg

❖ ❖ ❖

My philosophy is that life is all about learning and growing, and that life can be a real adventure of learning, growing, compassion, and joyfulness.

—John Mackey

❖ ❖ ❖

No one limits your growth but you. If you want to earn more, learn more. That means you'll work harder for a while; that means you'll work longer for a while. But you'll be paid for your extra effort with enhanced earnings down the road.

—Tom Hopkins

❖ ❖ ❖

Nothing we learn in this world is ever wasted.

—Eleanor Roosevelt

❖ ❖ ❖

One can choose to go back toward safety or forward toward growth. Growth must be chosen again and again; fear must be overcome again and again.

—Abraham Maslow

❖ ❖ ❖

Our business in life is not to get ahead of other people, but to get ahead of ourselves.

—Maltbie D. Matlock

❖ ❖ ❖

Our goal is long-term growth in revenue and absolute profit...so we invest aggressively in future innovation while tightly managing our short-term costs.

—Larry Page

❖ ❖ ❖

Our ideas, like orange-plants, spread out in proportion to the size of the box which imprisons the roots.

—Edward Bulwer Lytton

❖ ❖ ❖

Progress has not followed a straight ascending line, but

a spiral with rhythms of progress and retrogression, of evolution and dissolution.

—Johann Wolfgang von Goethe

❖ ❖ ❖

Some people are molded by their admirations, others by their hostilities.

—Elizabeth Bowen

❖ ❖ ❖

Strength and growth come only through continuous effort and struggle.

—Napoleon Hill

❖ ❖ ❖

The best rules to form a young man are: to talk little, to hear much, to reflect alone upon what has passed in company, to distrust one's own opinions, and value others that deserve it.

—Sir William Temple

❖ ❖ ❖

The fact is, that to do anything in the world worth doing, we must not stand back shivering and thinking of the cold and danger, but jump in and scramble through as well as we can.

—Robert Cushing

❖ ❖ ❖

The happiest life is that which constantly exercises and educates what is best in us.

—Hamerton

❖ ❖ ❖

The harvest of old age is the recollection and abundance of blessing previously secured.

—Marcus Tulius Cicero

The minute a man ceases to grow, no matter what his years, that minute he begins to be old.

—William James

❖ ❖ ❖

The most difficult thing in life is to know yourself.

—Thales

❖ ❖ ❖

The only journey is the journey within.

—Rainer Maria Rilke

❖ ❖ ❖

The only real mistake is the one from which we learn nothing.

—John Powell

❖ ❖ ❖

The organizational architecture is really that a centipede walks on hundred legs and one or two don't count. So if I lose one or two legs, the process will go on, the organization will go on, the growth will go on.

—Mukesh Ambani

❖ ❖ ❖

The perfecting of one's self is the fundamental base of all progress and all moral development.

—Confucius

❖ ❖ ❖

The purpose of learning is growth, and our minds, unlike our bodies, can continue growing as long as we live.

—Mortimer Adler

❖ ❖ ❖

The searching-out and thorough investigation of truth ought to be the primary study of man.

—Cicero

❖ ❖ ❖

The strongest principle of growth lies in human choice.

—George Eliot

❖ ❖ ❖

The unexamined life is not worth living.

—**Socrates**

❖ ❖ ❖

The way to gain a good reputation, is to endeavor to be what you desire to appear.

—**Socrates**

❖ ❖ ❖

There are no such things as limits to growth, because there are no limits to the human capacity for intelligence, imagination, and wonder.

—**Ronald Reagan**

❖ ❖ ❖

There is no discussion inside this boardroom to say we've got to get into this or that. We look at every growth opportunity on its merits.

—**James Packer**

❖ ❖ ❖

To conquer oneself is the best and noblest victory; to be vanquished by one's own nature is the worst defeat.

—**Plato**

❖ ❖ ❖

Today, many companies are reporting that their number one constraint on growth is the inability to hire workers with the necessary skills.

—**Bill Clinton**

❖ ❖ ❖

We all have to expand our capabilities to encompass the changing world, its growing diversity and, indeed, its complexity.

—**Lachlan Murdoch**

❖ ❖ ❖

We are either progressing or retrograding all the while; there is no such thing as remaining stationary in this life.

—James Freeman Clarke

❖ ❖ ❖

We are sometimes as different from ourselves as we are from others.

—Francois De La Rochefoucauld

❖ ❖ ❖

We call it infectious impatience. That's his hallmark and we are trying to inculcate it in the entire organization. Infectious impatience. So that things not only get done but get done in double quick time.

—Mukesh Ambani

❖ ❖ ❖

We don't think of ourselves as do-gooders or altruists. It's just that somehow we're trying our best to be run with some sense of moral compass even in a business environment that is growing.

—Craig Newmark

❖ ❖ ❖

We just have to go at 100 miles an hour in all our businesses, be they television broadcasting, be they magazine publishing, be they subscription television, be they online, be they gaming. We just have to go at one hundred miles an hour.

—James Packer

❖ ❖ ❖

We look at it as an opportunity to align our people, technology and investments against strategic growth targets.

—Trudy Muller

❖ ❖ ❖

We only become what we are by the radical and deep-seated refusal of that which others have made of us.

—Jean-Paul Sartre

❖ ❖ ❖

We started Yahoo in about April 1994. It started out as a way for us to keep track of things that we were interested in.

—David Filo

❖ ❖ ❖

We're just going to concentrate on what we've always done, which is to create the best possible online directory, adding content and other features along the way when it makes sense.

—Jerry Yang

❖ ❖ ❖

We're looking for something where we can make something happen: an industry where the competition is asleep, hasn't taken advantage. It's going to be hard to find another Blockbuster, but that doesn't mean you can't have three good companies growing. The point is, we're going to be busy.

—Wayne Huizenga

❖ ❖ ❖

What progress, you ask, have I made? I have begun to be a friend to myself.

—Hecato

❖ ❖ ❖

Who looks outside, dreams. Who looks inside, awakes.

—Jarl Jung

❖ ❖ ❖

Yes, know thyself: in great concerns or small, Be this thy care, for this, my friend, is all.

—Juvenal

❖ ❖ ❖

You don't learn to hold your own in the world by standing on guard, but by attacking and getting well hammered yourself.

—George Bernard Shaw

❖ ❖ ❖

You have to be willing to grow. Growth is different from something that happens to you: You produce it. You live it.

—Bruce Mau

❖ ❖ ❖

You will either step forward into growth or you will step back into safety.

—Abraham Maslow

❖ ❖ ❖

Your real influence is measured by your treatment of yourself.

—A. Bronson Alcott

❖ ❖ ❖

BUSINESS

A business exists to create a customer.

—Peter F. Drucker

❖ ❖ ❖

A business has to be involving, it has to be fun, and it has to exercise your creative instincts.

—Richard Branson

❖ ❖ ❖

A business like an automobile, has to be driven, in order to get results.

—B.C. Forbes

❖ ❖ ❖

A man should never neglect his family for business.

—Walt Disney

❖ ❖ ❖

An organization becomes bewildered rather than energized when it's asked to do too much at once.

—Michael Hammer and James Champy

❖ ❖ ❖

Being able to touch so many people through my businesses and make money while doing it, is a huge blessing.

—Magic Johnson

❖ ❖ ❖

Business has only two functions—marketing and innovation.

—Milan Kundera

❖ ❖ ❖

Business is more exciting than any game.

—Lord Beaverbrook

❖ ❖ ❖

Business opportunities are like buses, there's always another one coming.

—Richard Branson

❖ ❖ ❖

Business will get better, but we won't know when it does.

—Henry Ford

❖ ❖ ❖

Business, more than any other occupation, is a continual dealing with the future; it is a continual calculation, an instinctive exercise in foresight.

—Henry R. Luce

❖ ❖ ❖

Capital isn't that important in business. Experience isn't that important. You can get both of these things. What is important is ideas.

—Harvey S. Firestone

❖ ❖ ❖

Far and away the best prize that life offers is the chance to work hard at work, worth doing.

—Theodore Roosevelt

❖ ❖ ❖

For all of its faults, it gives most hardworking people a chance to improve themselves economically, even as the deck is stacked in favor of the privileged few. Here are the choices most of us face in such a system: Get bitter or get busy.

—Bill O' Reilly

❖ ❖ ❖

Good business leaders create a vision, articulate the vision, passionately own the vision, and relentlessly drive it to completion.

—Jack Welch

❖ ❖ ❖

Hire character. Train skill.

—Peter Schutz

I am not a fan of people who abuse service staff. In fact, I find it intolerable. Its an unpardonable sin as far as I'm concerned, taking out personal business or some other kind of dissatisfaction on a waiter or busboy.

—Anthony Michael

❖ ❖ ❖

I don't pay good wages because I have a lot of money; I have a lot of money because I pay good wages.

—Robert Bosch

❖ ❖ ❖

I feel that luck is a preparation meeting opportunity.

—Oprah Winfrey

❖ ❖ ❖

I had to make my own living and my own opportunity! But I made it! Don't sit down and wait for the opportunities to come. Get up and make them!

—C.J. Walker

❖ ❖ ❖

I have found no greater satisfaction than achieving success through honest dealing and strict adherence to the view that, for you to gain, those you deal with should gain as well.

—Alan Greenspan

❖ ❖ ❖

I like thinking big. If you're going to be thinking anything, you might as well think big.

—Donald Trump

❖ ❖ ❖

I wasn't satisfied just to earn a good living. I was looking to make a statement.

—Donald Trump

❖ ❖ ❖

If it really was a no-brainer to make it on your own in business there'd be millions of no-brained, hare-brained, and otherwise dubiously-brained individuals quitting their day jobs and hanging out their own shingles. Nobody would be left to round out the workforce and execute the business plan.

—Bill Rancic

❖ ❖ ❖

If there is such a thing as good leadership, it is to give by a good example.

—Ingvar Kamprad

❖ ❖ ❖

If you did not look after today's business then you might as well forget about tomorrow.

—Isaac Mophatlane

❖ ❖ ❖

If you don't make mistakes, you aren't really trying.

—Coleman Hawkins

❖ ❖ ❖

If you have always done it that way, it is probably wrong.

—Charles Kettering

❖ ❖ ❖

If you work just for money, you'll never make it, but if you love what you're doing and you always put the customer first, success will be yours.

—Ray Kroc

❖ ❖ ❖

In all realms of life, it takes courage to stretch your limits, express your power, and fulfill your potential. It's no different in the financial realm.

—Suze Orman

❖ ❖ ❖

In business, I've discovered that my purpose is to do my best to my utmost ability every day. That's my standard. I learned early in my life that I had high standards.

—Donald Trump

❖ ❖ ❖

In business, three things are necessary: knowledge, temper, and time.

—Owen Felltham

❖ ❖ ❖

In the business world, everyone is paid in two coins: cash and experience. Take the experience first; the cash will come later.

—Harold Geneen

❖ ❖ ❖

Industry is the soul of business and the keystone of prosperity.

—Charles Dickens

❖ ❖ ❖

It is difficult, but not impossible, to conduct strictly honest business.

—Mahatma Gandhi

❖ ❖ ❖

It is not the strongest of the species that survive, nor the most intelligent, but the one most responsive to change.

—Charles Darwin

❖ ❖ ❖

It takes more than capital to swing business. You've got to

have the A.I.D. degree to get by—Advertising, Initiative, and Dynamics.

—Ren Mulford Jr.

❖ ❖ ❖

It's through curiosity and looking at opportunities in new ways that we've always mapped our path at Dell. There's always an opportunity to make a difference.

—Michael Dell

❖ ❖ ❖

I've been in the business for 11 years I guess time flies when your having fun!

—William M. Kucmierowski

❖ ❖ ❖

Judge a man by his questions, not by his answers.

—Voltaire

❖ ❖ ❖

Leadership is a potent combination of strategy and character. But if you must be without one, be without the strategy.

—Norman Schwarzkopf

❖ ❖ ❖

Leadership is doing what is right when no one is watching.

—George van Valkenburg

❖ ❖ ❖

Leadership is the art of getting someone else to do something you want done because he wants to do it.

—Dwight Eisenhower

❖ ❖ ❖

Let every man be respected as an individual and no man idolized.

—Albert Einstein

❖ ❖ ❖

Let us not look back in anger or forward in fear, but around in awareness.

—James Thurber

❖ ❖ ❖

Let's be honest. There's not a business anywhere that is without problems. Business is complicated and imperfect. Every business everywhere is staffed with imperfect human beings and exists by providing a product or service to other imperfect human beings.

—Bob Parsons

❖ ❖ ❖

Life is too complicated not to be orderly.

—Martha Stewart

❖ ❖ ❖

Live daringly, boldly, fearlessly. Taste the relish to be found in competition—in having put forth the best within you.

—Henry J. Kaiser

❖ ❖ ❖

Long-range planning works best in the short term.

—Doug Evelyn

❖ ❖ ❖

Look well to this day. Yesterday is but a dream and tomorrow is only a vision. But today well lived makes every yesterday a dream of happiness and every tomorrow a vision of hope. Look well therefore to this day.

—Francis Gray

❖ ❖ ❖

Management is nothing more than motivating other people.

—Le Iacocca

❖ ❖ ❖

Managers and investors alike must understand that

accounting numbers are the beginning, not the end, of business valuation.

—Warren Edward Buffett

❖ ❖ ❖

Method is the very hinge of business, and there is no method without punctuality.

—Richard Cecil

❖ ❖ ❖

Motivation is the art of getting people to do what you want them to do because they want to do it.

—Dwight D. Eisenhower

❖ ❖ ❖

My son is now an 'entrepreneur'. That's what you're called when you don't have a job.

—Ted Turner

❖ ❖ ❖

No enterprise can exist for itself alone. It ministers to some great need, it performs some great service, not for itself, but for others...or failing therein, it ceases to be profitable and ceases to exist.

—Calvin Coolidge

❖ ❖ ❖

Nobody talks about entrepreneurship as survival, but that's exactly what it is and what nurtures creative thinking. Running that first shop taught me business is not financial science; it's about trading: buying and selling.

—Anita Roddick

❖ ❖ ❖

Our business in life is not to get ahead of others, but to get ahead of ourselves—to break our own records, to outstrip our yesterday by our today

—Stewart B. Johnson

❖ ❖ ❖

Our grand business undoubtedly is, not to see what lies dimly at a distance, but to do what lies clearly at hand.

—Thomas Carlyle

❖ ❖ ❖

Out there in some garage is an entrepreneur who's forging a bullet with your company's name on it.

—Gary Hamel

❖ ❖ ❖

Patience, persistence and perspiration make an unbeatable combination for success.

—Napoleon Hill

❖ ❖ ❖

Prophesy is a good line of business, but it is full of risks.

—Mark Twain

❖ ❖ ❖

Sometimes when you innovate, you make mistakes. It is best to admit them quickly and get on with improving your other innovations.

—Steve Jobs

❖ ❖ ❖

Speed is useful only if you are running in the right direction.

—Joel Barker

❖ ❖ ❖

Statistics suggest that when customers complain, business owners and managers ought to get excited about it. The complaining customer represents a huge opportunity for more business.

—Zig Ziglar

❖ ❖ ❖

Success in business requires training and discipline and hard work. But if you're not frightened by these things, the opportunities are just as great today as they ever were.

—David Rockefeller

❖ ❖ ❖

Success is often achieved by those who don't know that failure is inevitable.

—Coco Chanel

❖ ❖ ❖

Surely, no one will consider us lacking in reverence if we say that every one of the principles of modern salesmanship on which businessmen so much pride themselves, are brilliantly exemplified in Jesus' talk and work.

—Bruce Fairchild Barton

❖ ❖ ❖

Surviving a failure gives you more self-confidence. Failures are great learning tools...but they must be kept to a minimum.

—Jeffrey Immelt

❖ ❖ ❖

The absolute fundamental aim is to make money out of satisfying customers.

—John Egan

❖ ❖ ❖

The business of art is to enlarge and correct the heart and to lift our ideals out of the ugly and the mean through love of the ideal.... The business of art is to appeal to the soul.

—Florence Earle Coates

❖ ❖ ❖

The competitor to be feared is one who never bothers about you at all, but goes on making his own business better all the time.

—Henry Ford

❖ ❖ ❖

The cynic says, "One man can't do anything." I say, "Only one man can do anything."

—John W. Gardner

❖ ❖ ❖

The desire of knowledge, like the thirst for riches, increases ever with the acquisition of it.

—Laurence Sterne

❖ ❖ ❖

The enemy of the truth is very often not the lie—deliberate, contrived, and dishonest—but the myth-persistent, persuasive, and unrealistic.

—John F. Kennedy

❖ ❖ ❖

The entrepreneur always searches for change, responds to it, and exploits it as an opportunity.

—Peter F. Drucker

❖ ❖ ❖

The expectations of life depend upon diligence; the mechanic that would perfect his work must first sharpen his tools.

—Confucius

❖ ❖ ❖

The first one gets the oyster the second gets the shell.

—Andrew Carnegie

❖ ❖ ❖

The first rule of any technology used in a business is that automation applied to an efficient operation will magnify the efficiency. The second is that automation applied to an inefficient operation will magnify the inefficiency.

—Bill Gates

❖ ❖ ❖

The first rule of luck in business is that you should persevere in doing the right thing. Opportunities will come your way if you do.

—Ronald Cohen

❖ ❖ ❖

The golden rule for every businessman is this: Put yourself in your customer's place.

—Orison Swett Marden

❖ ❖ ❖

The good or ill of a man lies within his own will.

—Epictetus

❖ ❖ ❖

The great accomplishments of man have resulted from the transmission of ideas of enthusiasm.

—Thomas J. Watson

❖ ❖ ❖

The great leaders are like the best conductors—they reach beyond the notes to reach the magic in the players.

—Blaine Lee

❖ ❖ ❖

The important thing is not being afraid to take a chance. Remember, the greatest failure is to not try. Once you find something you love to do, be the best at doing it.

—Debbi Fields

❖ ❖ ❖

The man who does not work for the love of work but only for money is not likely to neither make money nor find much fun in life.

—Charles M. Schwab

❖ ❖ ❖

The man who will use his skill and constructive imagination to see how much he can give for a dollar, instead of how little he can give for a dollar, is bound to succeed.

—Henry Ford

❖ ❖ ❖

The minute you're satisfied with where you are, you aren't there anymore.

—Tony Gwynn

❖ ❖ ❖

The most serious mistakes are not being made as a result of wrong answers. The truly dangerous thing is asking the wrong question.

—Peter Drucker

❖ ❖ ❖

The new source of power is not money in the hands of a few, but information in the hands of many.

—John Naisbitt

❖ ❖ ❖

The noblest search is the search for excellence.

—Lyndon B. Johnson

❖ ❖ ❖

The only limits are, as always, those of vision.

—James Broughton

❖ ❖ ❖

The only way around is through.

—Robert Frost

❖ ❖ ❖

The success combination in business is: Do what you do better...and do more of what you do.

—David Joseph Schwartz

❖ ❖ ❖

The trick is in what one emphasizes. We either make ourselves miserable, or we make ourselves strong. The amount of work is the same.

—Carlos Castaneda

❖ ❖ ❖

The winners in life think constantly in terms of I can, I will, and I am. Losers, on the other hand, concentrate their waking thoughts on what they should have or would have done, or what they can't do.

—Dennis Waitley

❖ ❖ ❖

There are a lot of things that go into creating success. I don't like to do just the things I like to do. I like to do things that cause the company to succeed. I don't spend a lot of time doing my favorite activities.

—Michael Dell

❖ ❖ ❖

There is no royal, flower-strewn path to success. And if there is, I have not found it. For if I have accomplished anything in life, it is because I have been willing to work hard.

—C.J. Walker

❖ ❖ ❖

There is nothing so useless as doing efficiently that which should not be done at all.

—Peter Drucker

❖ ❖ ❖

They always say time changes things, but you actually have to change them yourself.

—Andy Warhol

❖ ❖ ❖

Time is the measure of business.

—Francis Bacon Sr.

❖ ❖ ❖

To be successful, you have to have your heart in your business, and your business in your heart.

—Thomas Watson Sr.

❖ ❖ ❖

To succeed in business, to reach the top, an individual must know all it is possible to know about that business.

—J. Paul Getty

❖ ❖ ❖

To succeed... you need to find something to hold on to, something to motivate you, something to inspire you.

—Tony Dorsett

❖ ❖ ❖

To the degree we're not living our dreams; our comfort zone has more control of us than we have over ourselves.

—Peter McWilliams

❖ ❖ ❖

To think creatively, we must be able to look afresh at what we normally take for granted.

—George Kneller

❖ ❖ ❖

To think is easy. To act is difficult. To act as one thinks is the most difficult.

—Johann Wolfgang von Goeth

❖ ❖ ❖

To waken interest and kindle enthusiasm is the sure way to teach easily and successfully.

—Tryon Edwards

❖ ❖ ❖

To win without risk is to triumph without glory.

—Pierre Corneille

❖ ❖ ❖

We are currently not planning on conquering the world.

—Sergey Brin

❖ ❖ ❖

Well, you know, I was a human being before I became a businessman.

—George Soros

❖ ❖ ❖

What helps people, helps business.

—Leo Burnett

❖ ❖ ❖

Whatever the mind of man can conceive and believe, it can achieve. Thoughts are things! And powerful things at that, when mixed with definiteness of purpose, and burning desire, can be translated into riches.

—Napoleon Hill

❖ ❖ ❖

Whenever you see a successful business, someone once made a courageous decision.

—Peter F. Drucker

❖ ❖ ❖

Where there is an open mind, there will always be a frontier.

—Charles F. Kettering

❖ ❖ ❖

Whether it's Google or Apple or free software, we've got some fantastic competitors and it keeps us on our toes.

—Bill Gates

❖ ❖ ❖

Whether you think you can or whether you think you can't, you're right!

—Henry Ford

❖ ❖ ❖

Who likes not his business, his business likes not him.

—William Hazlitt

❖ ❖ ❖

Why did I want to win? Because I didn't want to lose!

—Max Schmelling

❖ ❖ ❖

Winners take time to relish their work, knowing that scaling the mountain is what makes the view from the top so exhilarating.

—Denis Waitley

❖ ❖ ❖

Winning is not a sometime thing; it's an all time thing. You don't win once in a while, you don't do things right once in a while, you do them right all the time. Winning is habit. Unfortunately, so is losing.

—Vince Lombardi

❖ ❖ ❖

Yesterday's home runs don't win today's games.

—Babe Ruth

❖ ❖ ❖

You can fool all the people all the time if the advertising is right and the budget is big enough.

—Joseph E. Levine

❖ ❖ ❖

You must be the change, you wish to see in the world.

—Mahatma Gandhi

❖ ❖ ❖

You must either modify your dreams or magnify your skills.

—Jim Rohn

❖ ❖ ❖

You must remain focused on your journey to greatness.

—Les Brown

❖ ❖ ❖

You need to be aware of what others are doing, applaud their efforts, acknowledge their successes, and encourage them in their pursuits. When we all help one another, everybody wins.

—Jim Stovall

❖ ❖ ❖

You only have to do a very few things right in your life so long as you don't do too many things wrong.

—Warren Buffett

❖ ❖ ❖

You read a book from beginning to end. You run a business the opposite way. You start with the end, and then you do everything you must to reach it.

—Harold S. Geneen

❖ ❖ ❖

You've got to say, I think that if I keep working at this and want it badly enough I can have it. It's called perseverance.

—Lee Iacocca

❖ ❖ ❖

Your most unhappy customers are your greatest source of learning.

—Bill Gates

❖ ❖ ❖

ENTREPRENEURSHIP

A 'startup' is a company that is confused about – 1. What its product is. 2. Who its customers are. 3. How to make money?

—Dave McClure

❖ ❖ ❖

A lot of people have said that the Internet is a teenager. Guess who understands a teenager best: a teenager.

—Syed Balkhi

❖ ❖ ❖

A person who is quietly confident makes the best leader.

—Fred Wilson

❖ ❖ ❖

All humans are entrepreneurs not because they should start companies but because the will to create is encoded in human DNA.

—Reid Hoffman

❖ ❖ ❖

All of my friends were doing babysitting jobs. I wanted money without the job.

—Adam Horwitz

❖ ❖ ❖

All that you need to become an entrepreneur and change the world is a working brain—and pretty much nothing else.

—Adora Svitak

❖ ❖ ❖

Always deliver more than expected.

—Larry Page

❖ ❖ ❖

Always look for the fool in the deal. If you don't find one, it's you.

—Mark Cuban

❖ ❖ ❖

An invention that is quickly accepted will turn out to be a rather trivial alteration of something that has already existed.

—Edwin Land

❖ ❖ ❖

Anything that is measured and watched, improves.

—Bob Parsons

❖ ❖ ❖

As long as you're going to be thinking anyway, think big.

—Donald Trump

❖ ❖ ❖

Be undeniably good. No marketing effort or social media buzzword can be a substitute for that.

—Anthony Volodkin

❖ ❖ ❖

Before dreaming about the future or marking plans, you need to articulate what you already have going for you – as entrepreneurs do.

—Reid Hoffman

❖ ❖ ❖

Behold the turtle, he makes progress only when he sticks his neck out.

—Bruce Levin

❖ ❖ ❖

Best startups generally come from somebody needing to scratch an itch.

—Michael Arrington

❖ ❖ ❖

Data beats emotions.

—Sean Rad

❖ ❖ ❖

Design is not just what it looks like and feels like. Design is how it works.

—Steve Jobs

❖ ❖ ❖

Diligence is the mother of good luck.

—Benjamin Franklin

❖ ❖ ❖

Don't be afraid to assert yourself, have confidence in your abilities and don't let the bastards get you down.

—Michael Bloomberg

❖ ❖ ❖

Don't be cocky. Don't be flashy. There's always someone better than you.

—Tony Hsieh

❖ ❖ ❖

Don't limit yourself. Many people limit themselves to what they think they can do. You can go as far as your mind lets you. What you believe, remember, you can achieve.

—Mary Kay Ash

❖ ❖ ❖

Don't play games that you don't understand, even if you see lots of other people making money from them.

—Tony Hsieh

❖ ❖ ❖

Don't take too much advice. Most people who have a lot of advice to give—with a few exceptions—generalize whatever they did. Don't over-analyze everything. I myself have been guilty of over-thinking problems. Just build things and find out if they work.

—Ben Silbermann

❖ ❖ ❖

Don't try to be original, just try to be good.

—Paul Rand

❖ ❖ ❖

Don't worry about failure; you only have to be right once.

—Drew Houston

❖ ❖ ❖

Don't worry about funding if you don't need it. Today it's cheaper to start a business than ever.

—Noah Everett

❖ ❖ ❖

Don't worry about people stealing your design work. Worry about the day they stop.

—Jeffrey Zeldman

❖ ❖ ❖

Embrace what you don't know, especially in the beginning, because what you don't know can become your greatest asset. It ensures that you will absolutely be doing things different from everybody else.

—Sara Blakely

❖ ❖ ❖

Entrepreneur is someone who has a vision for something and a want to create.

—David Karp

❖ ❖ ❖

Even if you don't have the perfect idea to begin with, you can likely adapt.

—Victoria Ransom

❖ ❖ ❖

Every day that we spent not improving our products was a wasted day.

—Joel Spolsky

❖ ❖ ❖

Every single person I know who is successful at what they do is successful because they love doing it.

—Joe Penna

❖ ❖ ❖

Every time you state what you want or believe, you're the first to hear it. It's a message to both you and others about what you think is possible. Don't put a ceiling on yourself.

—Oprah Winfrey

❖ ❖ ❖

Everything started as nothing.

—Ben Weissenstein

❖ ❖ ❖

Fail often so you can succeed sooner.

—Tom Kelley

❖ ❖ ❖

Failures are the stepping stones to success.

—Farrhad Acidwalla

❖ ❖ ❖

Fearlessness is like a muscle. I know from my own life that the more I exercise it the more natural it becomes to not let my fears run me.

—Arianna Huffington

❖ ❖ ❖

Fortunes are built during the down market and collected in the up market.

—Jason Calacanis

❖ ❖ ❖

Get a mentor in the applicable field if you're at all unsure of what you're looking for.

—Kyle Bragger

❖ ❖ ❖

Get big quietly, so you don't tip off potential competitors.

—Chris Dixon

❖ ❖ ❖

Get five or six of your smartest friends in a room and ask them to rate your idea.

—Mark Pincus

❖ ❖ ❖

High expectations are the key to everything.

—Sam Walton

❖ ❖ ❖

I could never learn what I'm learning at college. They don't teach it there, because it can't be learned in that way.

—Philip Hartman

❖ ❖ ❖

I don't look to jump over 7-foot bars—I look for 1-foot bars that I can step over.

—Warren Buffett

❖ ❖ ❖

I don't think an economic slump will hurt good ideas.

—Rob Kalin

❖ ❖ ❖

I don't want to look too far ahead. The journey is what's happening right now, not what's on the finishing line.

—Sabirul Islam

❖ ❖ ❖

I doubt I'll ever go back to corporate work. Once you see the light, there is no turning back.

—Magnus Jepson

❖ ❖ ❖

I hope my companies will help create value and make people happier in the long run.

—Mark Bao

❖ ❖ ❖

I just try to think of myself as an entrepreneur who happens to be a teen.

—Mark Bao

❖ ❖ ❖

I knew that if I failed, I wouldn't regret that, but I knew the one thing I might regret is not trying.

—Jeff Bezos

❖ ❖ ❖

I like the idea of working hard now, so you can earn big later.

—Alex Fraiser

❖ ❖ ❖

I like to pride myself on thinking pretty long term, but not that long term.

—Mark Zuckerberg

❖ ❖ ❖

I never took a day off in my twenties. Not one.

—Bill Gates

❖ ❖ ❖

I think what teenagers lack is the belief that they can be unique and extraordinary in life. Make the most of your age because you're not going to be a teenager forever!

—Sabirul Islam

❖ ❖ ❖

Try not to make any decisions that I'm not excited about.

—Jake Nickell

❖ ❖ ❖

I would like to be the messed-up child of Steve Jobs, Mark Zuckerberg, Bill Gates, and Tim Ferriss morphed into super-genius entrepreneur.

—Marshall Haas

❖ ❖ ❖

I'm going to reinvent the wheel. My vision of the wheel is unique.

—King Sidharth

❖ ❖ ❖

Ideas are commodity. Execution of them is not.

—Michael Dell

❖ ❖ ❖

Ideas are easy. Implementation is hard.

—Guy Kawasaki

❖ ❖ ❖

If there's something you want to build, but the tech isn't there yet, just find the closest possible way to make it happen.

—Dennis Crowley

❖ ❖ ❖

If you are not embarrassed by the first version of your product, you've launched too late.

—Reid Hoffman

❖ ❖ ❖

If you can find people who think that what you're doing is great, they're going to do everything in their power to make it a success.

—Juliette Brindak

❖ ❖ ❖

If you can't communicate, you're going to find yourself a lonely businessperson.

—Keith J. Davis Jr.

❖ ❖ ❖

If you define yourself by how you differ from the competition, you're probably in trouble.

—Omar Hamoui

❖ ❖ ❖

If you have a goal, be relentless in your pursuit.

—Keith J. Davis Jr.

❖ ❖ ❖

If you just work on stuff that you like and you're passionate about, you don't have to have a master plan with how things will play out.

—Mark Zuckerberg

❖ ❖ ❖

If you pursued something that you felt strongly about, then I call that success.

—Adora Svitak

❖ ❖ ❖

If you're interested in the living heart of what you do, focus on building things rather than talking about them.

—Ryan Freitas

❖ ❖ ❖

If you're not a risk taker, you should get the hell out of business.

—Ray Kroc

❖ ❖ ❖

If you're not doing the things that you love, then your life is not worth living. What are you here for?

—King Sidharth

❖ ❖ ❖

If you're not in an uncomfortable situation every single day, then you're doing something wrong.

—Lauren Amarante

❖ ❖ ❖

If you're not making mistakes, then you're not making decisions.

—Catherine Cook

❖ ❖ ❖

If you're passionate about something and you work hard, then I think you will be successful.

—Pierre Omidyar

❖ ❖ ❖

In the end, a vision without the ability to execute it is probably a hallucination.

—Steve Case

❖ ❖ ❖

It was just one year ago that I realized that what I was doing was entrepreneurship. Just two weeks ago, I learned how to spell it [laughs].

—King Sidharth

❖ ❖ ❖

It's hard to do a really good job on anything you don't think about in the shower.

—Paul Graham

❖ ❖ ❖

It's more effective to do something valuable than to hope a logo or name will say it for you.

—Jason Cohen

❖ ❖ ❖

It's not about how many years of experience you have. It's about the quality of your years of experience.

—Jacob Cass

❖ ❖ ❖

It's not about ideas. It's about making ideas happen.

—Scott Belsky

❖ ❖ ❖

It's not that we need new ideas, but we need to stop having old ideas.

—Edwin Land

❖ ❖ ❖

Make every detail perfect and limit the number of details to perfect.

—Jack Dorsey

❖ ❖ ❖

Make it happen now, not tomorrow. Tomorrow is a loser's excuse.

—Andrew Fashion

❖ ❖ ❖

Manual labor sucks, dude.

—Alex Fraiser

❖ ❖ ❖

Money is like gasoline during a road trip. You don't want to run out of gas on your trip, but you're not doing a tour of gas stations.

—Tim O'Reilly

❖ ❖ ❖

No matter how brilliant your mind or strategy, if you're playing a solo game, you'll always lose out to a team.

—Reid Hoffman

❖ ❖ ❖

No more romanticizing about how cool it is to be an entrepreneur. It's a struggle to save your company's life—and your own skin—every day of the week.

—Spencer Fry

❖ ❖ ❖

Nothing works better than just improving your product.

—Joel Spolsky

❖ ❖ ❖

Risk more than others think is safe. Dream more than others think is practical.

—Howard Schultz

❖ ❖ ❖

See things in the present, even if they are in the future.

—Larry Ellison

❖ ❖ ❖

So often people are working hard at the wrong thing. Working on the right thing is probably more important than working hard.

—Caterina Fake

❖ ❖ ❖

Start today, not tomorrow. If anything, you should have started yesterday. The earlier you start, the more time you have to mess up.

—Emil Motycka

❖ ❖ ❖

Starting your own business is like riding a roller coaster. There are highs and lows and every turn you take is another twist. The lows are really low, but the highs can be really high. You have to be strong, keep your stomach tight, and ride along with the roller coaster that you started.

—Lindsay Manseau

❖ ❖ ❖

Stay self-funded as long as possible.

—Garrett Camp

❖ ❖ ❖

Success comes down to hard work plus passion, over time.

If you work really, really hard over a long period of time, it will pay off.

—Stanley Tang

❖ ❖ ❖

Sustaining a successful business is a hell of a lot of work, and staying hungry is half the battle.

—Wendy Tan White

❖ ❖ ❖

That's what I'm in it for.

—Mark Bao

❖ ❖ ❖

The biggest failure you can have in life is not trying at all.

—Emil Motycka

❖ ❖ ❖

The fastest way to change yourself is to hang out with people who are already the way you want to be.

—Reid Hoffman

❖ ❖ ❖

The hardest part about being an entrepreneur is that you'll fail ten times for every success.

—Adam Horwitz

❖ ❖ ❖

The last 10% it takes to launch something takes as much energy as the first 90%.

—Rob Kalin

❖ ❖ ❖

The most dangerous poison is the feeling of achievement. The antidote is to every evening think what can be done better tomorrow.

—Ingvar Kamprad

❖ ❖ ❖

The only thing worse than starting something and failing… is not starting something.

—Seth Godin

❖ ❖ ❖

The secret to successful hiring is this: look for the people who want to change the world.

—Marc Benioff

❖ ❖ ❖

The value of an idea lies in the using of it.

—Thomas Edison

❖ ❖ ❖

The way to get started is to quit talking and begin doing.

—Walt Disney

❖ ❖ ❖

Theory is splendid but until put into practice, it is valueless.

—James Cash Penney

❖ ❖ ❖

There is no reason to be hesitant…becoming an entrepreneur is a learning experience.

—Savannah Britt

❖ ❖ ❖

There's lots of bad reasons to start a company. But there's only one good, legitimate reason, and I think you know what it is: it's to change the world.

—Phil Libin

❖ ❖ ❖

There's no committee that says, "This is the type of person who can change the world—and you can't." Realizing that anyone can do it is the first step. The next step is figuring out how you're going to do it.

—Adora Svitak

❖ ❖ ❖

There's nothing wrong with staying small. You can do big things with a small team.

—Jason Fried

❖ ❖ ❖

Timing, perseverance, and ten years of trying will eventually make you look like an overnight success.

—Biz Stone

❖ ❖ ❖

To any entrepreneur: if you want to do it, do it now. If you don't, you're going to regret it.

—Catherine Cook

❖ ❖ ❖

Trust your instincts.

—Estee Lauder

❖ ❖ ❖

Turn a perceived risk into an asset.

—Aaron Patzer

❖ ❖ ❖

We are currently not planning on conquering the world.

—Sergey Brin

❖ ❖ ❖

We are really competing against ourselves, we have no control over how other people perform.

—Pete Cashmore

❖ ❖ ❖

What do you need to start a business? Three simple things: know your product better than anyone. Know your customer, and have a burning desire to succeed.

—Dave Thomas

❖ ❖ ❖

When I'm old and dying, I plan to look back on my life

and say "wow, that was an adventure," not "wow, I sure felt safe."

—Tom Preston-Werner

❖ ❖ ❖

When you find an idea that you just can't stop thinking about, that's probably a good one to pursue.

—Josh James

❖ ❖ ❖

Wonder what your customer really wants? Ask. Don't tell.

—Lisa Stone

❖ ❖ ❖

You always want to surround yourself with people who are rooting for you and who want you to succeed. Stay away from the naysayers who couldn't do it themselves.

—Arjun Rai

❖ ❖ ❖

You can't make anything viral, but you can make something good.

—Peter Shankman

❖ ❖ ❖

You could have a million ideas, but they're all worthless if you don't get them done.

—Lauren Amarante

❖ ❖ ❖

You don't learn to walk by following rules. You learn by doing and falling over.

—Richard Branson

❖ ❖ ❖

You don't need to have a 100-person company to develop that idea.

—Larry Page

❖ ❖ ❖

You jump off a cliff and you assemble an airplane on the way down.

—Reid Hoffman

❖ ❖ ❖

You just have to pay attention to what people need and what has not been done.

—Russell Simmons

❖ ❖ ❖

You shouldn't focus on why you can't do something, which is what most people do. You should focus on why perhaps you can, and be one of the exceptions.

—Steve Case

❖ ❖ ❖

You've got to stop doing all the things that people have tried, tested, and found out don't work.

—Michael Dunlop

❖ ❖ ❖

Your reputation is more important than your paycheck, and your integrity is worth more than your career.

—Ryan Freitas

❖ ❖ ❖

Your work is going to fill a large part of your life, and the only way to be truly satisfied is to do what you believe is great work. And the only way to do great work is to love what you do.

—Steve Jobs

❖ ❖ ❖

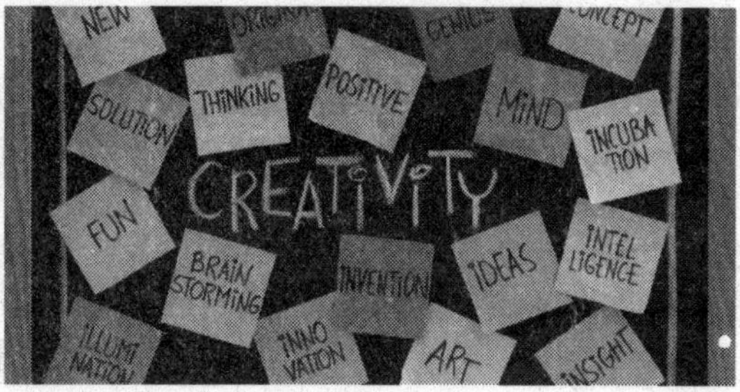

CREATIVITY: A NECESSITY

Balance suggests a perfect equilibrium. There is no such thing. That is a false expectation.... There are going to be priorities and dimensions of your life, how you integrate them is how you find true happiness.

—Denise Morrison

❖ ❖ ❖

I always did something that I was a little not ready to do. I think that, that is how you grow. When there's a moment of 'Wow, I'm not so sure that I can do this', and you push through those moments, it's then that you have a breakthrough. Sometimes that's a sign that something really great is about to happen. You're about to grow and learn a lot more about yourself.

—Marissa Mayer

❖ ❖ ❖

Identify your problems but give your power and energy to solutions.

—Tony Robbins

❖ ❖ ❖

The question I ask myself like almost every day is, 'Am I doing the most important thing I could be doing?'... Unless I feel like I'm working on the most important problem that I can help with, then I'm not going to feel good about how I'm spending my time. And that's what this company is.

—Mark Zuckerberg

❖ ❖ ❖

A creative mindset is in increasingly high demand: employers are vying for workers who are able to dream big and deliver big with the next must-have product. Creative thinking fuels innovation, it leads to new goods and services, creates jobs and delivers substantial economic rewards.

—Jim Hunt

❖ ❖ ❖

A discovery is said to be an accident meeting a prepared mind.

—Albert von Szent-Györgyi

❖ ❖ ❖

A new idea is delicate. It can be killed by a sneer or a yawn; it can be stabbed to death by a quip and worried to death by a frown on the right man's brow.

—Charles Brower

❖ ❖ ❖

A pile of rocks ceases to be a rock pile when somebody contemplates it with the idea of a cathedral in mind.

—Antoine Saint-Exupery

❖ ❖ ❖

All great deeds and all great thoughts have a ridiculous beginning.

—Albert Camus

❖ ❖ ❖

All human development, no matter what form it takes, must be outside the rules; otherwise we would never have anything new.

—Charles Kettering

❖ ❖ ❖

All things are created twice. There's a mental or first creation, and a physical or second creation to all things.

—Stephen Covey

❖ ❖ ❖

Anxiety is the hand maiden of creativity.

—Chuck Jones

❖ ❖ ❖

Big thinking precedes great achievement.

—Wilferd Peterson

❖ ❖ ❖

Change is the law of life and those who look only to the past or present are certain to miss the future.

—John F. Kennedy

❖ ❖ ❖

Creative thinking is not a talent, it is a skill that can be learnt. It empowers people by adding strength to their natural abilities which improves teamwork, productivity and where appropriate profits.

—Edward de Bono

❖ ❖ ❖

Creativity is inventing, experimenting, growing, taking risks, breaking rules, making mistakes, and having fun.

—Mary Lou Cook

❖ ❖ ❖

Creativity is not the finding of a thing, but the making something out of it after it is found.

—James Russell Lowell

❖ ❖ ❖

Discovery consists of seeing what everybody has seen and thinking what nobody has thought.

—Albert von Szent-Gyorgy

❖ ❖ ❖

Don't be afraid to take a big step when one is indicated. You can't cross a chasm in two small jumps.

—David Lloyd George

❖ ❖ ❖

Every act of creation is first of all an act of destruction.

—Picasso

❖ ❖ ❖

Everyone is a genius at least once a year. The real geniuses simply have their bright ideas closer together.

—Georg Christoph Lichtenberg

❖ ❖ ❖

Genius is infinite painstaking.

—Michelangelo

Genius is one percent inspiration, and ninety-nine percent perspiration.

—Thomas Edison

❖ ❖ ❖

Genius means little more than the faculty of perceiving in an unhabitual way.

—William James

❖ ❖ ❖

Great companies with the way they work, first start with great leaders.

—Steve Ballmer

❖ ❖ ❖

Great is the human who has not lost his child-like heart.

—Mencius

❖ ❖ ❖

High expectations are the key to absolutely everything.

—Sam Walton

❖ ❖ ❖

I am looking for a lot of people who have an infinite capacity not to know what can't be done.

—Henry Ford

❖ ❖ ❖

I think frugality drives innovation, just like other constraints do. One of the only ways to get out of a tight box is to invent your way out.

—Jeff Bezos

❖ ❖ ❖

Ideas are like rabbits. You get a couple and learn how to handle them, and pretty soon you have a dozen.

—John Steinbeck

❖ ❖ ❖

Ideas in secret die. They need light and air or they starve to death.

—Seth Godin

If I had asked people what they wanted, they would have said faster horses.

—Henry Ford

❖ ❖ ❖

If you always do what you always did, you will always get what you always got.

—Albert Einstein

❖ ❖ ❖

If you do not express your own original ideas, if you do not listen to your own being, you will have betrayed yourself.

—Rollo May

❖ ❖ ❖

If you do not the expect the unexpected, you will not find it, for it is not to be reached by search or trail.

—Heraclitus

❖ ❖ ❖

If you go to your grave without painting your masterpiece, it will not get painted. No one else can paint it.

—Gordon MacKenzie

❖ ❖ ❖

If you have always done it that way, it is probably wrong.

—Charles Kettering

❖ ❖ ❖

If you're changing the world, you're working on important things. You're excited to get up in the morning.

—Larry Page

❖ ❖ ❖

In the beginner's mind, there are many possibilities; in the expert's mind there are few.

—Shunryu Suzuki

❖ ❖ ❖

Innovation comes from the producer—not from the customer.

—W. Edwards Deming

❖ ❖ ❖

Innovation is serendipity, so you don't know what people will make.

—Tim Berners Lee

❖ ❖ ❖

Innovation is this amazing intersection between someone's imagination and the reality in which they live. The problem is, many companies don't have great imagination, but their view of reality tells them that it's impossible to do what they imagine.

—Ron Johnson

❖ ❖ ❖

Innovation opportunities do not come with the tempest but with the rustling of the breeze.

—Peter Drucker

❖ ❖ ❖

Insanity is doing the same thing over and over again but expecting different results.

—Albert Einstein

❖ ❖ ❖

Intuition will tell the thinking mind where to look next.

—Jonas Salk

❖ ❖ ❖

It is the essence of genius to make use of the simplest ideas.

—Charles Peguy

❖ ❖ ❖

It's easy to come up with new ideas; the hard part is letting go of what worked for you two years ago, but will soon be out of date.

—Roger von Oech

❖ ❖ ❖

It's not about having a specific set time; both personal and professional lives are 24/7. It's simply, more about making the right allocation to each one and recognizing that it's going to be different every single day.

—Ellen Kullman

❖ ❖ ❖

Lack of money is not an obstacle. Lack of an idea is.

—Ken Hakuta

❖ ❖ ❖

Life is fragile. We're not guaranteed a tomorrow so give it everything you've got.

—Tim Cook

❖ ❖ ❖

Man's mind, once stretched by a new idea, never regains its original dimensions.

—Oliver Wendell Holmes

❖ ❖ ❖

Mindless habitual behavior is the enemy of innovation.

—Rosabeth Moss Kanter

❖ ❖ ❖

Money never starts an idea; it is the idea that starts the money.

—William J. Cameron

❖ ❖ ❖

Necessity is the mother of invention.

—Anonymous

❖ ❖ ❖

Neither a lofty degree of intelligence, nor imagination, nor both together, go to the making of genius. Love, Love, Love. That is the soul of genius.

—Mozart

❖ ❖ ❖

No man can be successful, unless he first loves his work.

—David Sarnoff

❖ ❖ ❖

Nothing is more dangerous than a dogmatic worldview—nothing more constraining, more blinding to innovation, more destructive of openness to novelty.

—Stephen Jay Gould

❖ ❖ ❖

Nothing is more dangerous than an idea when it is the only one you have.

—Emile Chartier

❖ ❖ ❖

Once we rid ourselves of traditional thinking we can get on with creating the future.

—James Bertrand

❖ ❖ ❖

One of the challenges of innovation is figuring out how to wipe your mind clean about what you should be doing at any given moment, and not having a religious attachment to what's gotten you there thus far.

—Andrew Mason

❖ ❖ ❖

Some men look at things the way they are and ask why? I dream of things that are not and ask why not?

—Robert Kennedy

❖ ❖ ❖

The best thinking has been done in solitude. The worst has been done in turmoil.

—Thomas Edison

❖ ❖ ❖

The best vision is insight.

—Malcolm Forbes

❖ ❖ ❖

The best way to have a good idea is to have a lot of ideas.

—Dr. Linus Pauling

❖ ❖ ❖

The creation of something new is not accomplished by the intellect, but by the play instinct arising from inner necessity. The creative mind plays with the object it loves.

—Carl Jung

❖ ❖ ❖

The creative is the place where no one else has ever been. You have to leave the city of your comfort and go into the wilderness of your intuition. What you'll discover will be wonderful. What you'll discover is yourself.

—Alan Alda

❖ ❖ ❖

The creative person wants to be a know-it-all. He wants to know about all kinds of things: ancient history, nineteenth-century mathematics, current manufacturing techniques, flower arranging, and hog futures. Because he never knows when these ideas might come together to form a new idea. It may happen six minutes later or six months, or six years down the road. But he has faith that it will happen.

—Carl Ally

❖ ❖ ❖

The gift of fantasy has meant more to me than my talent for absorbing positive knowledge.

—Albert Einstein

❖ ❖ ❖

The greatest invention in the world is the mind of a child.

—Thomas Edison

❖ ❖ ❖

The heart and soul of a company is creativity and innovation.

—Robert Iger

❖ ❖ ❖

The impossible is often the untried.

—Jim Goodwin

❖ ❖ ❖

The most important single ingredient in the formula of success is knowing how to get along with people.

—Theodore Roosevelt

❖ ❖ ❖

The most potent muse of all is our own inner child.

—Stephen Nachmanovitch

❖ ❖ ❖

The only way to discover the limits of the possible is to go beyond them into the impossible.

—Arthur C. Clarke

❖ ❖ ❖

The silly question is the first intimation of some totally new development.

—Alfred North Whitehead

❖ ❖ ❖

The test of a first-rate intelligence is the ability to hold two opposed ideas in the mind at the same time, and still retain the ability to function.

—F. Scott Fitzgerald

❖ ❖ ❖

The uncreative mind can spot wrong answers, but it takes a very creative mind to spot wrong questions.

—Anthony Jay

❖ ❖ ❖

The world is but a canvas to the imagination.

—Henry David Thoreau

❖ ❖ ❖

The secret to successful hiring is this: look for the people who want to change the world.

—Marc Benioff

❖ ❖ ❖

There are no old roads to new directions.

—The Boston Consulting Group

❖ ❖ ❖

There is a vitality, a life force, that is translated to you into action, and because there is only one of you in all time, this expression is unique. And if you block it, it will never exist through any other medium, and will be lost.

—Martha Graham

❖ ❖ ❖

There is no doubt that creativity is the most important human resource of all. Without creativity, there would be no progress, and we would be forever repeating the same patterns.

—Edward de Bono

❖ ❖ ❖

To gain customer insights, we must understand that we are prisoners of what we know and what we believe.

—Mohanbir Sawhney

❖ ❖ ❖

To have a great idea, have a lot of them.

—Thomas Edison

❖ ❖ ❖

To raise new questions, new possibilities, to regard old problems from a new angle, requires creative imagination and marks real advance in science.

—Albert Einstein

❖ ❖ ❖

Vision is the art of seeing the invisible.

—Jonathan Swift

❖ ❖ ❖

We cannot solve a problem by using the same kind of thinking we used when we created them.

—Albert Einstein

❖ ❖ ❖

We have approximately 60,000 thoughts in a day. Unfortunately, 95% of them are thoughts we had the day before.

—Deepak Chopra

❖ ❖ ❖

We must not confuse distortion with innovation; distortion is useless change, art is a beneficial change.

—Chuck Jones

❖ ❖ ❖

What is now proved was once only imagined.

—William Blake

❖ ❖ ❖

When we all think alike, then no one is thinking.

—Walter Lippman

❖ ❖ ❖

When you innovate, you must prepare yourself for everybody to tell you that you're nuts.

—Larry Ellison

❖ ❖ ❖

Without passion, you don't have any energy, and without energy, you simply have nothing.

—Donald Trump

❖ ❖ ❖

Without the playing with fantasy no creative work has ever yet come to birth. The debt we owe to the play of imagination is incalculable.

—Carl Jung

❖ ❖ ❖

You don't need to be a genius or a visionary, or even a college graduate for that matter, to be successful. You just need framework and a dream.

—Michael Dell

❖ ❖ ❖

You don't understand anything unless you understand there are at least three ways.

—M. Minsky

❖ ❖ ❖

You must do the thing you think you cannot do.

—Eleanor Roosevelt

❖ ❖ ❖

PROFITABILITY

No man can tell if he is rich or poor by turning to his ledger. It is the heart that makes a man rich. He is rich according to what he is, not according to what he has.

—Henry Ward Beecher

❖ ❖ ❖

In the end, all business operations can be reduced to three words: people, product, and profits.

—Lee Iacoca

❖ ❖ ❖

A visionary company doesn't simply balance between idealism and profitability: it seeks to be highly idealistic and highly profitable. A visionary company doesn't simply balance between preserving a tightly held core ideology and stimulating vigorous change and movement; it does both to an extreme.

—Jim Collins

❖ ❖ ❖

In business, you're trying to make a buck. God was good to me and blessed me. I made some money and started this foundation years ago, and it has grown in size. With the foundation it's a lot different, because the bottom line isn't how you can make more money or get a better return, it's helping the projects that you feel strongly about move forward.

—Lee Iacoca

❖ ❖ ❖

I do not believe maximizing profits for the investors is the only acceptable justification for all corporate actions. The investors are not the only people who matter. Corporations can exist for purposes other than simply maximizing profits.

—John Mackey

❖ ❖ ❖

If your goal is anything but profitability—if it's to be big, or to grow fast, or to become a technology leader—you'll hit problems.

—Michael Porter

❖ ❖ ❖

Suppliers and especially manufacturers have market power because they have information about a product or a service that the customer does not and cannot have, and does not need if he can trust the brand. This explains the profitability of brands.

—Peter Drucker

❖ ❖ ❖

A business of high principle attracts high-caliber people more easily, thereby gaining a basic competitive and profit edge.

—Marvin Bower

❖ ❖ ❖

I don't want to do business with those who don't make a profit, because they can't give the best service.

—Richard Bach

❖ ❖ ❖

Make every thought, every fact, that comes into your mind pay you a profit. Make it work and produce for you. Think of things not as they are but as they might be. Don't merely dream—but create!

—Robert Collier

❖ ❖ ❖

Many receive advice, only the wise profit from it.

—Harper Lee

❖ ❖ ❖

Profit is not the legitimate purpose of business. The legitimate purpose of business is to provide a product or service that people need and do it so well that it's profitable.

—James Rouse

❖ ❖ ❖

One who works for his own profit is likely to work hard. One who works for the use of others, without profit to himself, is likely not to work any harder than he must.

—B. Carroll Reece

❖ ❖ ❖

The investor of today does not profit from yesterday's growth.

—Warren Buffett

❖ ❖ ❖

VISION

A clear vision, backed by definite plans, gives you a tremendous feeling of confidence and personal power.

—Brian Tracy

❖ ❖ ❖

A dream is your creative vision for your life in the future. You must break out of your current comfort zone and become comfortable with the unfamiliar and the unknown.

—Denis Waitley

❖ ❖ ❖

A journey of a thousand miles must begin with a single step.

—Lao Tsu

❖ ❖ ❖

A rock pile ceases to be a rock pile the moment a single man contemplates it, bearing within him the image of a cathedral.

—Antoine De Saint-Exupery

❖ ❖ ❖

A vision is not just a picture of what could be; it is an appeal to our better selves, a call to become something more.

—Rosabeth Moss Kanter

❖ ❖ ❖

Aim not for what you are, but for what you could be.

—Lucas Hellmer

❖ ❖ ❖

Better keep yourself clean and bright; you are the window through which you must see the world.

—George Bernard Shaw

❖ ❖ ❖

Capital isn't scarce; vision is.

—Sam Walton

❖ ❖ ❖

Cherish your visions; cherish your ideals; cherish the music that stirs in your heart, the beauty that forms in your mind, the loveliness that drapes your purest thoughts, for out of them will grow all delightful conditions, all, heavenly environment; of these, if you but remain true to them, your world will at last be built.

—James Allen

❖ ❖ ❖

Common sense is the knack of seeing things as they are, and doing things as they ought to be done.

—Harriet Beecher Stowe

❖ ❖ ❖

Determine that the thing can and shall be done and then we shall find the way.

—Abraham Lincoln

❖ ❖ ❖

Dreams are extremely important. You can't do it unless you can imagine it.

—George Lucas

❖ ❖ ❖

Efforts and courage are not enough without purpose and direction.

—John F. Kennedy

❖ ❖ ❖

Every age needs men who will redeem the time by living with a vision of the things that are to be.

—Adlai E. Stevenson

❖ ❖ ❖

Every creator painfully experiences the chasm between his inner vision and its ultimate expression.

—Isaac Bashevis Singer

❖ ❖ ❖

Faith is taking the first step even when you don't see the whole staircase.

—Martin Luther King, Jr.

❖ ❖ ❖

Faith is to believe what you do not yet see; the reward for this faith is to see what you believe.

—St. Augustine

❖ ❖ ❖

Formulate and stamp indelibly on your mind a mental picture of yourself as succeeding. Hold this picture tenaciously. Never permit it to fade. Your mind will seek to develop the picture.

—Norman Vincent Peale

❖ ❖ ❖

He who cherishes a beautiful vision, a lofty ideal in his heart, will one day realize it.

—James Allen

❖ ❖ ❖

How you look at it is pretty much how you'll see it.

—Rasheed Ogunlaru

❖ ❖ ❖

I can teach anybody how to get what they want out of life. The problem is that I can't find anybody who can tell me what they want.

—Mark Twain

❖ ❖ ❖

I saw the angel in the marble and carved until I set him free.

—Michelangelo

❖ ❖ ❖

I skate to where the puck is going to be, not where it is going.

—Wayne Gretsky

❖ ❖ ❖

I would give all the wealth of the world, and all the deeds of all the heroes, for one true vision.

—Henry David Thoreau

❖ ❖ ❖

If you are working on something exciting that you really care about, you don't have to be pushed. The vision pulls you.

—Steve Jobs

❖ ❖ ❖

If you go as far as you can see, you will then see enough to go even farther.

—John Wooden

❖ ❖ ❖

Imagination gives you the picture. Vision gives you the impulse to make the picture your own.

—Robert Collier

❖ ❖ ❖

Inside yourself or outside, you never have to change what you see, only the way you see it.

—Thaddeus Golas

❖ ❖ ❖

Instead of thinking about where you are, think about where you want to be. It takes twenty years of hard work to become an overnight success.

—Diana Rankin

❖ ❖ ❖

It is a terrible thing to see and have no vision.

—Helen Keller

❖ ❖ ❖

It is always wise to look ahead, but difficult to look farther than you can see.

—Winston Churchill

❖ ❖ ❖

It is the familiar that usually eludes us in life. What is before our nose is what we see last.

—William Barrett

❖ ❖ ❖

It takes someone with a vision of the possibilities to attain new levels of experience. Someone with the courage to live his dreams.

—Les Brown

❖ ❖ ❖

It's lack of faith that makes people afraid of meeting challenges, and I believe in myself.

—Muhammad Ali

❖ ❖ ❖

Knowing your destination is half the journey.

—Anonoymous

❖ ❖ ❖

Leaders establish the vision for the future and set the strategy for getting there; they cause change. They motivate and inspire others to go in the right direction and they, along with everyone else, sacrifice to get there.

—John Kotter

❖ ❖ ❖

Leaders must invoke an alchemy of great vision.

—Henry Kissinger

❖ ❖ ❖

Leadership is the capacity to translate vision into reality.

—Warren Bennis

❖ ❖ ❖

Learn to see, and then you'll know that there is no end to the new worlds of our vision.

—Carlos Castaneda

❖ ❖ ❖

Life is the movie you see through your own eyes.

—Denis Waitley

❖ ❖ ❖

Look well to this day. Yesterday is but a dream and tomorrow is only a vision. But today well lived makes every yesterday a dream of happiness and every tomorrow a vision of hope. Look well therefore to this day.

—Francis Gray

❖ ❖ ❖

Make no little plans. They have no magic to stir men's blood and probably themselves will not be realized. Make big plans. Aim high in hope and work. Remembering that a noble, logical diagram once recorded will not die.

—Daniel H. Burnham

❖ ❖ ❖

Make sure you visualize what you really want, not what someone else wants for you.

—Jerry Gillies

❖ ❖ ❖

Many a times an opportunity is lost because a man is out looking for four-leaf clovers.

—Anonymous

❖ ❖ ❖

Most people are not really free. They are confined by the niche in the world that they carve out for themselves. They limit themselves to fewer possibilities by the narrowness of their vision.

—V. S. Naipaul

❖ ❖ ❖

My interest is in the future because I am going to spend the rest of my life there.

—Charles Kettering

❖ ❖ ❖

Nothing stops an organization faster than people who believe that the way you worked yesterday is the best way to work tomorrow.

—Jon Madonna

❖ ❖ ❖

Obstacles are those frightful things you see when you take your eyes off your goal.

—Henry Ford

❖ ❖ ❖

Only he who can see the invisible can do the impossible.

—Frank Gaines

❖ ❖ ❖

Only those who can see the invisible can accomplish the impossible!

—Patrick Snow

❖ ❖ ❖

Our job is not to set things right but to see them right.

—Eric Butterworth

❖ ❖ ❖

Our main business is not to see what lies dimly at a distance, but to do what lies clearly at hand.

—Thomas Carlyle

❖ ❖ ❖

Our thoughts take the wildest flight; even at the moment when they should arrange themselves in thoughtful order.

—Lord Byron

❖ ❖ ❖

Seeing yourself as you want to be is the key to personal growth.

—Anonymous

❖ ❖ ❖

So many of our dreams seem impossible, then improbable, then inevitable.

—Christopher Reeve

❖ ❖ ❖

The assumption that what currently exists must necessarily exist is the acid that corrodes all visionary thinking.

—Murray Bookchin

❖ ❖ ❖

The eye sees only what the mind is prepared to comprehend.

—Henri Bergson

❖ ❖ ❖

The first step towards creating an improved future is developing the ability to envision it.

—Anonymous

❖ ❖ ❖

The future belongs to the people who see possibilities before they become obvious.

—Ted Levitt

❖ ❖ ❖

The job of the artist is always to deepen the mystery.

—Francis Bacon

❖ ❖ ❖

The master observes the world but trusts his inner vision.

—Lao-tzu

❖ ❖ ❖

The mind is its own place, and in itself, can make heaven of Hell, and a hell of Heaven.

—John Milton

❖ ❖ ❖

The only limits are, as always, those of vision.

—James Broughton

❖ ❖ ❖

The real voyage of discovery consists of not in seeking new landscapes but in having new eyes.

—Marcel Proust

❖ ❖ ❖

The very essence of leadership is that you have to have vision. It's got to be a vision you articulate clearly and forcefully on every occasion. You can't blow an uncertain trumpet.

—Father Theodore Hesburgh

❖ ❖ ❖

The wisest keeps something of the vision of a child. Though he may understand a thousand things that a child could not understand, he is always a beginner, close to the original meaning of life.

—John Macy

❖ ❖ ❖

The wisest men follow their own direction.

—Euripides

❖ ❖ ❖

There are many paths to the top of the mountain, but the view is always the same.

—Chinese Proverb

❖ ❖ ❖

There is nothing more difficult for a truly creative painter than to paint a rose, because before he can do so he has first to forget all the roses that were ever painted.

—Henri Matisse

❖ ❖ ❖

Throughout the centuries, there were men who took first steps, down new roads, armed with nothing but their own vision.

—Ayn Rand

❖ ❖ ❖

To be a successful entrepreneur, one needs a vision of greatness for one's work. If we dream extravagantly, we will be inspired to forge a reality beyond the straight jacket of practicalities. There is a profound connection between art and enterprise which allows businesses to overcome the limitations of their existing visions.

—Sir Ernest Hall

❖ ❖ ❖

To believe in the things you can see and touch is no belief at all. But to believe in the unseen is both a triumph and a blessing.

—Bob Proctor

❖ ❖ ❖

To grasp and hold a vision, that is the very essence of successful leadership—not only on the movie set where I learned it, but everywhere.

—Ronald Reagan

❖ ❖ ❖

To see things in the seed, that is genius.

—Lao Tsu

❖ ❖ ❖

Vision is not enough. It must be combined with venture. It is not enough to stare up the steps, we must step up the stairs.

—Vaclav Havel

❖ ❖ ❖

Vision looks inward and becomes duty. Vision looks outward and becomes aspiration. Vision look upward and becomes faith.

—Stephen S. Wise

❖ ❖ ❖

Vision without a task is only a dream. A task without a vision is but drudgery. But vision with a task is a dream fulfilled.

—Anonymous

❖ ❖ ❖

Vision without an action is merely a dream. Action without vision just passes the time. Vision with action can change the world.

—Joel A. Barker

❖ ❖ ❖

Vision without execution is hallucination.

—Thomas Edison

❖ ❖ ❖

Visualize the thing you want. See it, feel it, believe in it. Make your mental blueprint and begin.

—Robert Collier

❖ ❖ ❖

We can chart our future clearly and wisely only when we know the path which has led to the present.

—Adlai E. Stevenson

❖ ❖ ❖

We do not need more of the things that are seen, we need more of the things that are unseen.

—Calvin Coolidge

❖ ❖ ❖

We go where our vision is.

—Joseph Edward Murphy

❖ ❖ ❖

We lift ourselves by our thoughts. We climb upon our vision of ourselves. If you want to enlarge your life, you must first enlarge your thought of it and of yourself. Hold the ideal of yourself as you long to be, always everywhere.

—Orison Swett Marden

❖ ❖ ❖

We must act on what we know. I take as my guide the hope of a saint: In crucial things, unity; in important things, diversity; in all things, generosity.

—George Herbert Walker Bush

❖ ❖ ❖

We will build new ships to carry man forward into the universe, to gain a new foothold on the moon, and to prepare for new journeys to worlds beyond our own.

—George Herbert Walker Bush

❖ ❖ ❖

What we see depends mainly on what we look for.

—John Lubbock

❖ ❖ ❖

When you have a sense of your own identity and a vision of where you want to go in your life, you then have the basis for reaching out to the world and going after your dreams for a better life.

—Stedman Graham

❖ ❖ ❖

When you have vision, it affects your attitude. Your attitude is optimistic rather than pessimistic.

—Charles R. Swindoll

❖ ❖ ❖

Where there is no vision, there is no hope.

—George Washington Carver

❖ ❖ ❖

You have to see the pattern, understand the order and experience the vision.

—Gerber

❖ ❖ ❖

This is the gist of all worship—to be pure and to do well to other.

—Swami Vivekananda

❖ ❖ ❖

You've got to think about big things while you're doing small things, so that all the small things go in the right direction.

—Alvin Toffler

❖ ❖ ❖

Your vision will become clear only when you can look into your own heart. Who looks outside, dreams; who looks inside, awakens.

—Carl Jung

❖ ❖ ❖

INNOVATION

Well the protester, I think, is a very powerful thing. It's basically a mechanism of democracy that, along with capitalism, scientific innovation, those things have built the modern world. And it's wonderful that the new tools have empowered that protester so that state secrets, bad developments are not hidden anymore.

—Bill Gates

❖ ❖ ❖

There is no innovation and creativity without failure, Period.

—Brene Brown

❖ ❖ ❖

Business has only two functions – marketing and innovation.

—Milan Kundera

❖ ❖ ❖

Learning and innovation go hand in hand. The arrogance of success is to think that what you did yesterday will be sufficient for tomorrow.

—William Pollard

❖ ❖ ❖

I cannot help fearing that men may reach a point where they look on every new theory as a danger, every innovation as a toilsome trouble, every social advance as a first step toward revolution, and that they may absolutely refuse to move at all.

—Alexis de Tocqueville

❖ ❖ ❖

Without tradition, art is a flock of sheep without a shepherd. Without innovation, it is a corpse.

—Winston Churchill

❖ ❖ ❖

Imagination is not only the uniquely human capacity to envision that which is not, and therefore the fount of all invention and innovation. In its arguably most transformative and revelatory capacity, it is the power to that enables us to empathize with humans whose experiences we have never shared.

—J.K. Rowling

❖ ❖ ❖

I'm not against screens, or new songs, or innovation. I just don't like the gimmicks. I want to know when worship is over that that leader's sole purpose was to glorify the Lord Jesus Christ.

—Charles R. Swindoll

❖ ❖ ❖

Governments will always play a huge part in solving big problems. They set public policy and are uniquely able to provide the resources to make sure solutions reach everyone who needs them. They also fund basic research, which is a crucial component of the innovation that improves life for everyone.

—Bill Gates

❖ ❖ ❖

Cutting the deficit by gutting our investments in innovation and education is like lightening an overloaded airplane by removing its engine. It may make you feel like you're flying high at first, but it won't take long before you feel the impact.

—Barack Obama

❖ ❖ ❖

I'm a big fan of small business ownership. I think it's the backbone of American innovation. But to be successful, you first have to have the courage to go for it.

—Bill Rancic

❖ ❖ ❖

I believe in innovation and that the way you get innovation is you fund research and you learn the basic facts.

—Bill Gates

❖ ❖ ❖

Innovation is the specific instrument of entrepreneurship. The act that endows resources with a new capacity to create wealth.

—Peter Drucker

❖ ❖ ❖

Innovation is taking two things that already exist and putting them together in a new way.

—Tom Freston

❖ ❖ ❖

Success doesn't necessarily come from breakthrough innovation but from flawless execution. A great strategy alone won't win a game or a battle; the win comes from basic blocking and tackling.

—Naveen Jain

❖ ❖ ❖

People acting in their own self-interest is the fuel for all the discovery, innovation, and prosperity that powers the world.

—John Stossel

❖ ❖ ❖

An important scientific innovation rarely makes its way by gradually winning over and converting its opponents: What does happen is that the opponents gradually die out.

—Max Planck

❖ ❖ ❖

Most of us understand that innovation is enormously important. It's the only insurance against irrelevance. It's the only guarantee of long-term customer loyalty. It's the only strategy for out-performing a dismal economy.

—Gary Hamel

❖ ❖ ❖

Innovation is hard. It really is. Because most people don't get it. Remember, the automobile, the airplane, the telephone, these were all considered toys at their introduction because they had no constituency. They were too new.

—Nolan Bushnell

❖ ❖ ❖

Innovation by definition will not be accepted at first. It takes repeated attempts, endless demonstrations, monotonous rehearsals before innovation can be accepted and internalized by an organization. This requires 'courageous patience'.

—Warren Bennis

❖ ❖ ❖

The world is moving so fast these days that the man who says it can't be done is generally interrupted by someone doing it.

—Elbert Hubbard

❖ ❖ ❖

A business has to be evolving, it has to be fun, and it has to exercise your creative interests.

—Richard Branson

❖ ❖ ❖

Don't worry about people stealing an idea. If it's original, you will have to ram it down their throats.

—Howard Aiken

❖ ❖ ❖

Large corporations welcome innovation and individualism in the same way the dinosaurs welcomed large meteors.

—Dilbert Comic Strip

❖ ❖ ❖

If it's a good idea, go ahead and do it. It is much easier to apologise than it is to get permission.

—Grace Hopper

❖ ❖ ❖

MARKETING

If you're attacking your market from multiple positions and your competition isn't, you have all the advantage and it will show up in your increased success and income.

—Jay Abraham

❖ ❖ ❖

Understand that you need to sell you and your ideas in order to advance your career, gain more respect, and increase your success, influence and income.
The fact is, everyone is in sales. Whatever area you work in, you do have clients and you do need to sell.

—Jay Abraham

❖ ❖ ❖

No matter what your product is, you are ultimately in the education business. Your customers need to be constantly educated about the many advantages of doing business with you, trained to use your products more effectively, and taught how to make never-ending improvement in their lives.

—Robert G. Allen

❖ ❖ ❖

If you do build a great experience, customers tell each other about that. Word of mouth is very powerful.

—Jeff Bezos

❖ ❖ ❖

The aim of marketing is to know and understand the

customer so well the product or service fits him and sells itself.

—Peter Drucker

❖ ❖ ❖

A market is never saturated with a good product, but it is very quickly saturated with a bad one.

—Henry Ford

❖ ❖ ❖

I don't take myself seriously all the time; I have to do quirky things, such as helping football teams, moving the ball away from McAllister's foot, getting into The Sun and The Star—because, you know, I like sensationalism, it's a part of what I do.

—Uri Geller

❖ ❖ ❖

It's a very, very tough market. So unless you do a really good job, you buy the right products from the manufacturers, you service the customer, they keep coming back, they bring their friends in, it's all about numbers, numbers, numbers.

—John Ilhan

❖ ❖ ❖

We react very quickly in the market. We can make quick changes.

—John Ilhan

❖ ❖ ❖

This may seem simple, but you need to give customers what they want, not what you think they want. And, if you do this, people will keep coming back.

—John Ilhan

❖ ❖ ❖

A lot of companies have chosen to downsize, and maybe that was the right thing for them. We chose a different path.

Our belief was that if we kept putting great products in front of customers, they would continue to open their wallets.

—Steve Jobs

❖ ❖ ❖

Give a man a fish and he will eat for a day. Teach a man to fish and he will eat for a lifetime. Teach a man to create an artificial shortage of fish and he will eat steak.

—Jay Leno

❖ ❖ ❖

Our success is a direct result of knowing how to market a brand and having the right people representing the brand.

—Greg Norman

❖ ❖ ❖

Don't blame the marketing department. The buck stops with the chief executive.

—John D. Rockefeller

❖ ❖ ❖

Next to doing the right thing, the most important thing is to let people know you are doing the right thing.

—John D. Rockefeller

❖ ❖ ❖

Don't bring your need to the marketplace, bring your skill. If you don't feel well, tell your doctor, but not the marketplace. If you need money, go to the bank, but not the marketplace.

—Jim Rohn

❖ ❖ ❖

Customers don't always know what they want. The decline in coffee-drinking was due to the fact that most of the coffee people bought was stale and they weren't enjoying it. Once they tasted ours and experienced what we call the third place...a gathering place between home and work where they were treated with respect...they found we were filling a need they didn't know they had.

—Howard Schultz

❖ ❖ ❖

The point to remember about selling things is that, as well as creating atmosphere and excitement around your products, you've got to know what you're selling.

—Stuart Wilde

❖ ❖ ❖

The greatest enemy of a good plan is the dream of a perfect plan.

—Carl von Clausewitz

❖ ❖ ❖

As long as I have failed to defeat my enemy, I must fear that he will defeat me; therefore I am not in sole control; he controls me just as I control him.

—Carl von Clausewitz

❖ ❖ ❖

Try not to become a man of success but rather try to be a man of value.

—Albert Einstein

❖ ❖ ❖

Either write something worth reading or do something worth writing.

—Benjamin Franklin

❖ ❖ ❖

Great wisdom not applied to action and behavior is meaningless data.

—Peter Drucker

❖ ❖ ❖

Advertising is a tax for having an unremarkable product.

—Robert Stephens

❖ ❖ ❖

If you want to understand how a lion hunts, don't go to the zoo. Go to the jungle.

—Jim Stengel

❖ ❖ ❖

The purest treasure mortal times can afford is a spotless reputation.

—William Shakespeare

❖ ❖ ❖

It is not the strongest of the species that survive, nor the most intelligent, but the one most responsive to change.

—Charles Darwin

❖ ❖ ❖

The aim of marketing is to know and understand the customer so well that the product or service fits him and sells itself.

—Peter F. Drucker

❖ ❖ ❖

The sole purpose of marketing is to sell more to more people, more often and at higher prices. There is no other reason to do it.

—Sergio Zyman

❖ ❖ ❖

Don't find customers for your products, find products for your customers.

—Seth Godin

❖ ❖ ❖

What really decides consumers to buy or not to buy is the content of your advertising, not its form.

—David Ogilvy

❖ ❖ ❖

Instead of one-way interruption, web marketing is about

delivering useful content at precisely the right moment when a buyer needs it.

—David Meerman Scott

❖ ❖ ❖

The aim of marketing is to make selling superfluous.

—Peter Drucker

❖ ❖ ❖

If you have more money than brains you should focus on outbound marketing. If you have more brains than money, you should focus on inbound marketing.

—Guy Kawasaki

❖ ❖ ❖

Marketing wants 'Mr. Right' but Sales but wants 'Mr. Right Now'.

—Anonymous

❖ ❖ ❖

Markets are conversations.

—Levine, Locke, Searls and Weinberger

❖ ❖ ❖

Content is King!

—Bill Gates

❖ ❖ ❖

What helps people, helps business.

—Leo Burnett

❖ ❖ ❖

Marketing takes a day to learn. Unfortunately, it takes a lifetime to master.

—Phil Kolter

❖ ❖ ❖

Advertising in the final analysis should be news. If it is not news, it is worthless.

—Adolph Ochs

❖ ❖ ❖

The aim of marketing is to get customers to know, like and trust you.

—Anonymous

❖ ❖ ❖

A powerful global conversation has begun. Through the Internet, people are discovering and inventing new ways to share relevant knowledge with blinding speed. As a direct result, markets are getting smarter—and getting smarter faster than most companies.

—Levine, Locke, Searls and Weinberger

❖ ❖ ❖

CUSTOMER RELATIONSHIP MANAGEMENT

Customer satisfaction is worthless. Customer loyalty is priceless.

—Jeffrey Gitomer

❖ ❖ ❖

Lot of companies have chosen to downsize, and maybe that was the right thing for them. We chose a different paths. Our belief was that if we kept putting great products in front of customers, they would continue to open their wallets.

—Steve Jobs

❖ ❖ ❖

If you work just for money, you'll never make it, but if you love what you're doing and you always put the customer first, success will be yours.

—Ray Krock

❖ ❖ ❖

For us, our most important stakeholder is not our stockholders, it is our customers. We're in business to serve the needs and desires of our core customer base.

—John Mackey

❖ ❖ ❖

If you love your customer to death, you can't go wrong.

—Graham Day

❖ ❖ ❖

We see our customers as invited guests to a party, and we are the hosts. It's our job every day to make every important aspect of the customer experience a little bit better.

—Jeff Bezos

❖ ❖ ❖

You've got to look for a gap, where competitors in a market have grown lazy and lost contact with the readers or the viewers.

—Rupert Murdoch

❖ ❖ ❖

In our way of working, we attach a great deal of importance to humility and honesty. With respect for human values, we promise to serve our customers with integrity.

—Azim Premji

❖ ❖ ❖

Don't try to tell the customer what he wants. If you want to be smart, be smart in the shower. Then get out, go to work and serve the customer!

—Gene Buckley

❖ ❖ ❖

The most important adage and the only adage is, the customer comes first, whatever the business, the customer comes first.

—Kerry Stokes

❖ ❖ ❖

Customer service is just a day in, day out ongoing, never ending, unremitting, persevering, compassionate, type of activity.

—Leon Gorman

❖ ❖ ❖

Every company's greatest assets are its customers, because without customers there is no company.

—Michael LeBoeuf

❖ ❖ ❖

Excellent firms don't believe in excellence—only in constant improvement and constant change.

—Tom Peters

❖ ❖ ❖

Friendly makes sales—and friendly generates repeat business.

—Jeffrey Gitomer

❖ ❖ ❖

Service, in short, is not what you do, but who you are. It is a way of living that you need to bring to everything you do, if you are to bring it to your customer interactions.

—Betsy Sanders

❖ ❖ ❖

Every contact we have with a customer influences whether or not they'll come back. We have to be great every time or we'll lose them.

—Kevin Stirtz

❖ ❖ ❖

Here is a simple but powerful rule: always give people more than what they expect to get.

—Nelson Boswell

❖ ❖ ❖

Customers today want the very most and the very best for the very least amount of money, and on the best terms. Only the individuals and companies that provide absolutely excellent products and services at absolutely excellent prices will survive.

—Brian Tracy

❖ ❖ ❖

It helps a ton when you learn people's names and don't butcher them when trying to pronounce them.

—Jerry Yang

❖ ❖ ❖

I don't do business with those who don't make a profit because they can't give the best service.

—Richard Bach

❖ ❖ ❖

If you don't genuinely like your customers, chances are they won't buy.

—Thomas Watson

❖ ❖ ❖

Merely satisfying customers will not be enough to earn their loyalty. Instead, they must experience exceptional service worthy of their repeat business and referral. Understand the factors that drive this.

—Elbert Hubbard

❖ ❖ ❖

Men are rich only as they give. He who gives great service gets great rewards.

—Elbert Hubbard

❖ ❖ ❖

Mission statement about treating people with respect and dignity is not just words but a creed we live by every day. You can't expect your employees to exceed the expectations of your customers if you don't exceed the employees' expectations of management.

—Howard Schultz

❖ ❖ ❖

People expect good service but few are willing to give it.

—Robert Gateley

❖ ❖ ❖

Revolve your world around the customer and more customers will revolve around you.

—Heather Williams

❖ ❖ ❖

The customer's perception is your reality.

—Kate Zabriskie

❖ ❖ ❖

Do what you do so well that they will want to see it again and bring their friends.

—Walt Disney

❖ ❖ ❖

The longer you wait, the harder it is to produce outstanding customer service.

—William H. Davidow

❖ ❖ ❖

The single most important thing to remember about any enterprise is that there are no results inside its walls. The result of a business is a satisfied customer.

—Peter Drucker

❖ ❖ ❖

When the customer comes first, the customer will last.

—Robert Half

❖ ❖ ❖

Right or wrong, the customer is always right.

—Marshall Field

❖ ❖ ❖

Under promise and over deliver.

—Toby Bloomberg

❖ ❖ ❖

Profit in business comes from repeat customers; customers that boast about your product and service, and that bring friends with them.

—W. Edwards Deming

❖ ❖ ❖

Your customer doesn't care how much you know until they know how much you care.

—Damon Richards

❖ ❖ ❖

Every client you keep, is one less that you need to find.

—Nigel Sanders

❖ ❖ ❖

If you make customers unhappy in the physical world, they might each tell six friends. If you make customers unhappy on the Internet, they can each tell 6,000 friends.

—Jeff Bezos

❖ ❖ ❖

The purpose of a business is to create a customer who creates customers.

—Shiv Singh

❖ ❖ ❖

It's much harder to provide a great customer service than I would have ever realised. It's much more art than science in some of these other areas and not just about the facts but about how you are conveying them.

—David Yu

❖ ❖ ❖

Nothing is so contagious as enthusiasm.

—Samuel Taylor Coleridge

❖ ❖ ❖

Only a life lived in the service to others is worth living.

—Albert Einstein

❖ ❖ ❖

Good customer service costs less than bad customer service.

—Sally Gronow, Welsh Water

❖ ❖ ❖

Whether you are big or small, you cannot give good

customer service if your employees don't feel good about coming to work.

—Martin Oliver

❖ ❖ ❖

If we keep doing what we're doing, we're going to keep getting what we're getting.

—Stephen Covey

❖ ❖ ❖

Everyone in an organisation should be involved with customer service, not only are they feeling the customer but they are getting a feeling for what's not working.

—Penny Handscomb

❖ ❖ ❖

We don't want to push our ideas on to customers, we simply want to make what they want.

—Laura Ashley

❖ ❖ ❖

A little experience often upsets a lot of theory.

—S. Parkes Cadman

❖ ❖ ❖

Whatever your business is, talk to your customers and provide them with what they want. It makes sense.

—Robert Bowman

❖ ❖ ❖

You are serving a customer, not a life sentence. Learn how to enjoy your work.

—Laurie McIntosh

❖ ❖ ❖

Your best customers leave quite an impression. Do the same, and they won't leave at all.

—SAP Ad

❖ ❖ ❖

Unless you have 100% customer satisfaction...you must improve.

—Horst Schulz

❖ ❖ ❖

It starts with respect. If you respect the customer as a human being, and truly honor their right to be treated fairly and honestly, everything else is much easier.

—Doug Smith

❖ ❖ ❖

An ounce of loyalty is worth a pound of cleverness.

—Elbert Hubbard

❖ ❖ ❖

Worry about being better; bigger will take care of itself. Think one customer at a time and take care of each one the best way you can.

—Gary Comer

❖ ❖ ❖

Consumers are statistics. Customers are people.

—Stanley Marcus

❖ ❖ ❖

TEAMWORK

Teamwork is the ability to work together toward a common vision. The ability to direct individual accomplishment toward organizational objectives. It is the fuel that allows common people to attain uncommon results.

—Andrew Carnegie

❖ ❖ ❖

In union, there is strength.

—Aesop

❖ ❖ ❖

A team is more than a collection of people. It is a process of give and take.

—Barbara Glacel & Emile Robert Jr.

❖ ❖ ❖

Gettin' good players is easy. Gettin' 'em to play together is the hard part.

—Casey Stengel

❖ ❖ ❖

Coming together is a beginning. Keeping together is progress. Working together is success.

—Henry Ford

❖ ❖ ❖

In teamwork, silence isn't golden, it's deadly.

—Mark Sanborn

❖ ❖ ❖

Never doubt that a small group of thoughtful citizens can change the world. Indeed, it is the only thing that ever has.

—Margaret Mead

❖ ❖ ❖

Teamwork: Simply stated, it is less me and more we.

—Anonymous

❖ ❖ ❖

If you can laugh together, you can work together.

—Robert Orben

❖ ❖ ❖

Talent wins games, but teamwork and intelligence wins championships.

—Michael Jordan

❖ ❖ ❖

T—Together, E—Everyone, A—Achieves, M- More.

—Chambless

❖ ❖ ❖

Team player: Once who unites others toward a shared destiny through sharing information and ideas, empowering others and developing trust.

—Dennis Kinlaw

❖ ❖ ❖

Teamwork divides the task and double the success.

—Anonymous

❖ ❖ ❖

Teamwork is working together—even when apart.

—Anonymous

❖ ❖ ❖

Alone we can do so little. Together we can do so much.

—Helen Keller

❖ ❖ ❖

There is no 'i' in team but there is in win.

—Michael Jordan

❖ ❖ ❖

I'm not under too much of an illusion of how smart or un-smart I am because film-making ultimately is about teamwork.

—Guy Ritchie

❖ ❖ ❖

The main ingredient of stardom is the rest of the team.

—John Wooden

❖ ❖ ❖

A team is where a boy can prove his courage on his own. A gang is where a coward goes to hide.

—Mickey Mantle

❖ ❖ ❖

The speed of the boss is the speed of the team.

—Lee Iacocca

❖ ❖ ❖

The strength of the team is each individual member. The strength of each member is the team.

—Phil Jackson

❖ ❖ ❖

Either we're a team or we aren't. Either you trust me or you don't.

—Ally Carter

❖ ❖ ❖

To collaborative team members, completing one another is more important than competing with one another.

—John C. Maxwell

❖ ❖ ❖

I love teamwork. I love the idea of everyone rallying together to help me win.

—Jarod Kintz

❖ ❖ ❖

With an enthusiastic team you can achieve almost anything.

—Tahir Shah

❖ ❖ ❖

No matter the disappointment, you simply cannot divorce your favorite team.

—Kevin Walker

❖ ❖ ❖

Teamwork makes the dream work.

—Anonymous

❖ ❖ ❖

A leader must inspire or his team will expire.

—Orrin Woodward

❖ ❖ ❖

Teachers call it copying...we call it teamwork!

—Anonymous

❖ ❖ ❖

Only by binding together as a single force will we remain strong and unconquerable.

—Chris Bradford

❖ ❖ ❖

Teamwork begins by building trust. And the only way to do that is to overcome our need for invulnerability.

—Patrick Lencions

❖ ❖ ❖

Trust is knowing that when a team member pushes you, they are doing it because they care about the team.
Great teams do not hold back with one another. They

are unafraid to air their dirty laundry. They admit their mistakes, their weaknesses, and their concerns without fear of reprisal.

—Patrick Lencioni

❖ ❖ ❖

Teamwork is the secret that makes common people achieve uncommon results.

—Ifeanyi Enoch Onuoha

❖ ❖ ❖

If two men on the same job agree all the time, one is useless. If they disagree all the time, both are useless.

—Darryl F. Zanuck

❖ ❖ ❖

It doesn't take strength to win. It takes the true heart of the team to win.

—Emily Voyles

❖ ❖ ❖

You need to be aware of what others are doing, applaud their efforts, acknowledge their successes, and encourage them in their pursuits. When we all help one another, everybody wins.

—Jim Stovall

❖ ❖ ❖

It is not a question of how well each process works, the question is how well they all work together.

—Lloyd Dobens

❖ ❖ ❖

Build for your team a feeling of oneness, of dependence on one another and of strength to be derived by unity.

—Vince Lombardi

❖ ❖ ❖

There is no such thing as a self-made man. You will reach your goals only with the help of others.

—George Shinn

❖ ❖ ❖

Respect your fellow human being, treat them fairly, disagree with them honestly, enjoy their friendship, explore your thoughts about one another candidly, work together for a common goal and help one another achieve it.

—Bill Bradley

❖ ❖ ❖

Great teamwork is the only way we create the breakthroughs that define our careers.

—Pat Riley

❖ ❖ ❖

If everyone is moving forward together, then success takes care of itself.

—Henry Ford

❖ ❖ ❖

When a team outgrows individual performance and learns team confidence, excellence becomes a reality.

—Joe Paterno

❖ ❖ ❖

Individual commitment to a group effort—that is what makes a team work, a company work, a society work, a civilization work.

—Vince Lombardi

❖ ❖ ❖

The nice thing about teamwork is that you always have others on your side.

—Margaret Carty

❖ ❖ ❖

No problem is insurmountable. With a little courage, teamwork and determination a person can overcome anything.

—Anonymous

❖ ❖ ❖

People who work together will win, whether it be against complex football defences, or the problems of modern society.

—Vince Lombardi

❖ ❖ ❖

When a gifted team dedicates itself to unselfish trust and combines instinct with boldness and effort, it is ready to climb.

—Patanjali

❖ ❖ ❖

The secret is to work less as individuals and more as a team. As a coach, I play not my eleven best, but my best eleven.

—Knute Rockne

❖ ❖ ❖

Your most precious possession is not your financial assets. Your most precious possession is the people you have working there, and what they carry around in their heads, and their ability to work together.

—Robert Reich

❖ ❖ ❖

Many hands make light work.

—John Heywood

❖ ❖ ❖

No person will make a great business who wants to do it all himself or get all the credit.

—Andrew Carnegie

❖ ❖ ❖

"It is literally true that you can succeed best and quickest by helping others to succeed."

—Napoleon Hill

❖ ❖ ❖

Individual commitment to a group effort—that is what makes a team work.

—Vincent Lombardi

❖ ❖ ❖

Treat a person as he is, and he will remain as he is. Treat him as he could be, and he will become what he should be.

—Jimmy Johnson

❖ ❖ ❖

A job worth doing is worth doing together.

—Anonymous

❖ ❖ ❖

A group becomes a team when each member is sure enough of himself and his contribution to praise the skills of the others.

—Norman Shidle

❖ ❖ ❖

A successful team is a group of many hands but of one mind.

—Bill Bethel

❖ ❖ ❖

Always treat your employees exactly as you want them to treat your best customers

—Stephen R. Covey

❖ ❖ ❖

As a team leader, create teams who: Care, Cooperate & are Committed.

—Anonymous

❖ ❖ ❖

A creative man is motivated by the desire to achieve, not by the desire to beat others.

—Ayn Rand

❖ ❖ ❖

Do you want a collection of brilliant minds or a brilliant collection of minds?

—R. Meredith Belbin

❖ ❖ ❖

Synergy—the bonus that is achieved when things work together harmoniously.

—Mark Twain

❖ ❖ ❖

Team members who feel threatened but who are not aware of it become rigid—and that stops teamwork' will.

—Schutz

❖ ❖ ❖

Teams share the burden and divide the grief.

—Doug Smith

❖ ❖ ❖

Teamwork is the lynchpin in our long term success.

—Ned Lautenbach

❖ ❖ ❖

The best job goes to the person who can get it done without passing the buck or coming back with excuses.

—Napoleon Hill

❖ ❖ ❖

The path to greatness is along with others.

—Baltasar Gracion

❖ ❖ ❖

The whole is greater than the sum of the parts.

—Kurt Koffka

❖ ❖ ❖

The achievements of an organization are the results of the combined effort of each individual.

—Vince Lombardi

❖ ❖ ❖

When your team is winning, be ready to be tough, because winning can make you soft. On the other hand, when you team is losing, stick by them. Keep believing."

—Bo Schembechler

❖ ❖ ❖

Individuals play the game, but teams beat the odds."

—SEAL Team

❖ ❖ ❖

If a team is to reach its potential, each player must be willing to subordinate his personal goals to the good of the team.

—Bud Wilkinson

❖ ❖ ❖

People have been known to achieve more as a result of working with others than against them.

—Dr. Allan Fromme

❖ ❖ ❖

When he took time to help the man up the mountain, he scaled it himself.

—Tibetan Proverb

❖ ❖ ❖

In order to become a leading home run hitter, a batter must be surrounded by good hitters, otherwise, the pitchers will 'pitch around' him. Likewise, many successful people became that way from being on a good team.

—Laing Burns Jr.

❖ ❖ ❖

Teamwork is neither 'good' nor 'desirable'. It is a fact. Wherever people work together or play together they do so as a team. Which team to use for what purpose is a crucial, difficult and risky decision that is even harder to unmake. Managements have yet to learn how to make it.

—Peter F. Drucker

❖ ❖ ❖

If we were all determined to play the first violin we should never have an ensemble. Therefore, respect every musician in his proper place.

—Robert Schumann

❖ ❖ ❖

Many of us are more capable than some of us...but none of us is as capable as all of us!!

—Tom Wilson

❖ ❖ ❖

Good teams incorporate teamwork into their culture, creating the building blocks for success.

—Ted Sundquist

❖ ❖ ❖

No one can whistle a symphony. It takes a whole orchestra to play it.

—H.E. Luccock

❖ ❖ ❖

The ratio of We's to I's is the best indicator of the development of a team.

—Lewis B. Ergen

❖ ❖ ❖

So powerful is the light of unity that it can illuminate the whole earth.

—Bahá'u'lláh

❖ ❖ ❖

A group becomes a team when each member is sure enough of himself and his contribution to praise the skills of others.

—Norman Shidle

❖ ❖ ❖

Teamwork: A few harmless flakes working together can unleash an avalanche of destruction.

—Justin Sewell

❖ ❖ ❖

Strategy is not a solo sport, even if you're the CEO.

—Max McKeown

❖ ❖ ❖

Individually, we are one drop. Together, we are an ocean.

—Ryunosuke Satoro

❖ ❖ ❖

Sticks in a bundle are unbreakable.

—Proverb

❖ ❖ ❖

A boat doesn't go forward if each one is rowing their own way.

—Proverb

❖ ❖ ❖

One piece of log creates a small fire, adequate to warm you up, add just a few more pieces to blast an immense bonfire, large enough to warm up your entire circle of friends; needless to say that individuality counts but teamwork dynamites.

—Jin Kwon

❖ ❖ ❖

Cooperation is the thorough conviction that nobody can get there unless everybody gets there.

—Virginia Burden

❖ ❖ ❖

A single leaf working alone provides no shade.

—Chuck Page

❖ ❖ ❖

A snowflake is one of God's most fragile creations, but look what they can do when they stick together!

—**Anonymous**

❖ ❖ ❖

It is a fact that in the right formation, the lifting power of many wings can achieve twice the distance of any bird flying alone.

—**Anonymous**

❖ ❖ ❖

If I have seen further than others, it is by standing upon the shoulders of giants.

—**Isaac Newton**

❖ ❖ ❖

BRAND BUILDING

Unless you have absolute clarity of what your brand stands for, everything else is irrelevant.

—Mark Baynes

❖ ❖ ❖

The first step to brand success, no matter what the category of brand, is being able to establish a simple and meaningful point of difference that you'll be able to embed in peoples' minds, or make 'sticky'.

—Allen Adamson

❖ ❖ ❖

The three key rules of marketing are brand recognition, brand recognition, brand recognition.

—Anonymous

❖ ❖ ❖

A brand is not a product or a promise or a feeling. It's the sum of all the experiences you have with a company.

—Amir Kassaei

❖ ❖ ❖

A brand for the company is like a reputation for a person. You earn reputation by trying to do hard things well.

—Jeff Bezos

❖ ❖ ❖

A brand is a living entity—and it is enriched or undermined

cumulatively over time, the product of a thousand small gestures.

—Michael Eisner

❖ ❖ ❖

Your brand is created out of customer contact and the experience your customers have of you.

—Stelios Haji-Ioannou

❖ ❖ ❖

A brand is the proprietary visual, emotional, rational and cultural image that you associate with a company or product.

—Charles R. Pettis

❖ ❖ ❖

Products are made in the factory, but brands are created in the mind.

—Walter Landor

❖ ❖ ❖

Brands are the express checkout for people living their lives at ever-increasing speed.

—Brandweek

❖ ❖ ❖

Brands are decision-making shortcuts in a world of people like you looking for shortcuts.

—Harry Beckwith

❖ ❖ ❖

Your brand is what people say about you when you're not in the room.

—Jeff Bezos

❖ ❖ ❖

A product can be quickly outdated, but a successful brand is timeless.

—Stephen King

❖ ❖ ❖

SALES

Whenever an individual or a business decides that success has been attained, progress stops.

—**Thomas J. Watson Jr.**

❖ ❖ ❖

Everyone is in business for himself, for he is selling his services, labor or ideas. Until one realizes that this is true he will not take conscious charge of his life and will always be looking outside himself for guidance.

—**Sidney Madwed**

❖ ❖ ❖

You've got to be success minded. You've got to feel that things are coming your way when you're out selling; otherwise, you won't be able to sell anything.

—**Curtis Carlson**

❖ ❖ ❖

It used to be that people needed products to survive. Now products need people to survive.

—**Nicholas Johnson**

❖ ❖ ❖

Art is making something out of nothing and selling it.

—**Frank Zappa**

❖ ❖ ❖

Sell your cleverness and buy bewilderment. Cleverness is mere opinion. Bewilderment brings intuitive knowledge.

—Jalal Uddin Rumi

❖ ❖ ❖

Advertising is, actually, a simple phenomenon in terms of economics. It is merely a substitute for a personal sales force—an extension, if you will, of the merchant who cries aloud his wares.

—Rosser Reeves

❖ ❖ ❖

Catch a man a fish, and you can sell it to him. Teach a man to fish, and you ruin a wonderful business opportunity.

—Karl Marx

❖ ❖ ❖

Of course you sell candidates for political office the same way you sell soap or sealing wax or whatever; because, when you get right down to it, that's the only way anything is sold.

—Sid Bernstein

❖ ❖ ❖

When buying and selling are controlled by legislation, the first things to be bought and sold are legislators.

—P.J. O' Rourke

❖ ❖ ❖

Our job is to sell our clients' merchandise...not ourselves. Our job is to kill the cleverness that makes us shine instead of the product. Our job is to simplify, to tear away the unrelated, to pluck out the weeds that are smothering the product message.

—William Bernbach

❖ ❖ ❖

The successful people are the ones who can think up things for the rest of the world to keep busy at.

—Don Marquis

❖ ❖ ❖

Most people think 'selling' is the same as 'talking'. But the most effective salespeople know that listening is the most important part of their job.

—Roy Bartell

❖ ❖ ❖

All progress is based upon a universal innate desire of every organism to live beyond its income.

—Samuel Butler

❖ ❖ ❖

There is no such thing as a self-made man. We are made up of thousands of others. Everyone who has ever done a kind deed for us, or spoken one word of encouragement to us, has entered into the makeup of our character and our thoughts, as well as our success.

—George Matthew Adams

❖ ❖ ❖

On any given Monday I am one sale closer and one idea away from being a Millionaire.

—Larry D. Turner

❖ ❖ ❖

Quality isn't something that can be argued into an article or promised into it. It must be put there. If it isn't put there, the finest sales talk in the world won't act as a substitute.

—C.G. Campbell

❖ ❖ ❖

The first thing one must do to succeed in advertising is to have the attention of the reader. That means to be interesting. The next thing is to stick to the truth, and that means rectifying whatever's wrong in the merchant's business. If the truth isn't tellable, fix it so it is. That is about all there is to it.

—John E. Powers

❖ ❖ ❖

I have learned that trying to guess what the boss or the client wants is the most debilitating of all influences in the creation of good advertising.

—Leo Burnett

❖ ❖ ❖

As you travel down life's highway...whatever be your goal, you cannot sell a doughnut without acknowledging the hole.

—Harold J. Shayler

❖ ❖ ❖

The spectator-buyer is meant to envy herself as she will become if she buys the product. She is meant to imagine herself transformed by the product into an object of envy for others, an envy which will then justify her loving herself. One could put this another way: the publicity image steals her love of herself as she is, and offers it back to her for the price of the product.

—John Berger

❖ ❖ ❖

Every sale has five basic obstacles: no need, no money, no hurry, no desire, no trust.

—Zig Ziglar

❖ ❖ ❖

Money is good for bribing yourself through the inconveniences of life.

—Gottfried Reinhardt

❖ ❖ ❖

Every memorable act in the history of the world is a triumph of enthusiasm. Nothing great was ever achieved without it because it gives any challenge or any occupation, no matter how frightening or difficult, a new meaning. Without enthusiasm you are doomed to a life of mediocrity but with it you can accomplish miracles.

—Og Mandino

❖ ❖ ❖

Success is the culmination of failures, mistakes, false starts, confusion, and the determination to keep going anyway.

—Nick Gleason

❖ ❖ ❖

Business is like riding a bicycle. Either you keep moving or you fall down.

—Frank Lloyd Wright

❖ ❖ ❖

The most unprofitable item ever manufactured is an excuse.

—John Mason

❖ ❖ ❖

Commercial society regards people as bundles of appetites, a conception that turns human beings inside out, leaving nothing to be regarded as inherently private. Commercial society finds unintelligible the idea that anything—an emotion, activity, or product—is too 'intimately personal' for uninhibited commercial treatment.

—George Will

❖ ❖ ❖

1% of repeat purchases are made out of indifference and not out of loyalty.

—Industry analysts

❖ ❖ ❖

We succeed in enterprises which demand the positive qualities we possess, but we excel in those which can also make use of our defects.

—Alexis de Tocqueville

❖ ❖ ❖

To speak and to speak well are two things. A fool may talk, but a wise man speaks.

—Ben Jonson

❖ ❖ ❖

If you are not taking care of your customer, your competitor will.

—Bob Hooey

❖ ❖ ❖

Sales are contingent upon the attitude of the salesman, not the attitude of the prospect.

—William Clement Stone

❖ ❖ ❖

A wise man is cured of ambition by ambition itself; his aim is so exalted that riches, office, fortune and favour cannot satisfy him.

—Samuel Johnson

❖ ❖ ❖

Enthusiasm is the inspiration of everything great. Without it no man is to be feared, and with it none despised.

—Christian Nestell Bovee

❖ ❖ ❖

Negotiating techniques do not work all that well with kids, because in the middle of a negotiation, they will say something completely unrelated such as, 'You know what? I have a belly button!' and completely throw you off guard.

—Bo Bennett

❖ ❖ ❖

Eloquence, at its highest pitch, leaves little room for reason or reflection, but addresses itself entirely to the desires and affections, captivating the willing hearers, and subduing their understanding.

—David Hume

❖ ❖ ❖

The secret of man's success resides in his insight into the moods of people, and his tact in dealing with them.

—J.G. Holland

❖ ❖ ❖

Only in our dreams are we free. The rest of the time we need wages.

—Terry Pratchett

❖ ❖ ❖

How you think when you lose determines how long it will be until you win.

—Gilbert K. Chesterton

❖ ❖ ❖

What helps luck is a habit of watching for opportunities, of having a patient but restless mind, of sacrificing one's ease or vanity, or uniting a love of detail to foresight, and of passing through hard times bravely and cheerfully.

—Victor Cherbuliez

❖ ❖ ❖

If we had no winter, the spring would not be so pleasant: if we did not sometimes taste of adversity, prosperity would not be so welcome.

—Josh Billings

❖ ❖ ❖

In order to succeed, we must first believe that we can.

—Nikos Kazantzakis

❖ ❖ ❖

Nobody counts the number of ads you run; they just remember the impression you make.

—William Bernbach

❖ ❖ ❖

You don't close a sale, you open a relationship if you want to build a long-term, successful enterprise.

—Patricia Fripp

❖ ❖ ❖

Everyone lives by selling something.

—Robert Louis Stevenson

❖ ❖ ❖

"Beginning is not only a kind of action. It is also a frame of mind, a kind of work, an attitude, a consciousness.

—Edward Said

❖ ❖ ❖

A mediocre idea that generates enthusiasm will go further than a great idea that inspires no one.

—Mary Kay Ash

❖ ❖ ❖

People don't ask for facts in making up their minds. They would rather have one good, soul-satisfying emotion than a dozen facts.

—Robert Keith Leavitt

❖ ❖ ❖

I have never worked a day in my life without selling. If I believe in something, I sell it, and I sell it hard.

—Estée Lauder

❖ ❖ ❖

It's just called 'The Bible' now. We dropped the word 'Holy' to give it a more mass-market appeal.

—Hodder & Stoughton

❖ ❖ ❖

It used to be that people needed products to survive. Now products need people to survive.

—Nicholas Johnson

❖ ❖ ❖

If you work just for money, you'll never make it. But if you love what you are doing, and always put the customer first, success will be yours.

—Ray Kroc

❖ ❖ ❖

A smart salesperson listens to emotions not facts.

—Anonymous

❖ ❖ ❖

Victory is sweetest when you've known defeat.

—Malcolm Forbes

❖ ❖ ❖

Day by day, what you do is who you become.

—Heraclitus

❖ ❖ ❖

The wise man puts himself last and finds himself first.

—Lao Tsu

❖ ❖ ❖

Good ideas are common—what's uncommon are people who will work hard enough to bring them about.

—Ashleigh Brilliant

❖ ❖ ❖

Falling down is how we grow. Staying down is how we die.

—**Brian Vaszily**

❖ ❖ ❖

Life is like riding a bicycle. To keep your balance, you must keep moving.

—**Albert Einstein**

❖ ❖ ❖

The difference between involvement and commitment is like ham and eggs. The chicken is involved; the pig is committed.

—**Martina Navratilova**

❖ ❖ ❖

RELATIONSHIP

The only rock I know that stays steady and the only institution I know that works is the Family.

—Lee Lacocca

❖ ❖ ❖

Other things may change us, but we start and end with the family.

—Anthony Brandt

❖ ❖ ❖

When you look at your life, the greatest happiness's are family happiness's.

—Joyce Brothers

❖ ❖ ❖

You don't choose your family. They are God's gift to you, as you are to them.

—Desmond Tutu

❖ ❖ ❖

Relationship is an art. The dream that two people create is more difficult to master than one.

—Don Miguel Ruiz

❖ ❖ ❖

A partner is someone who makes you more than you are, simply by being by your side.

—Albert Kim

❖ ❖ ❖

If you were going to die soon and had only one phone call you could make, who would you call and what would you say? And why are you waiting?

—Stephen Levine

❖ ❖ ❖

To know when to go away and when to come closer is the key to any lasting relationship.

—Doménico Cieri Estrada

❖ ❖ ❖

It is usually the case that people who knows you better than you know yourself think you're a pretty good person.

—Robert Brault

❖ ❖ ❖

Once you find someone to share your ups and downs, downs are almost as good as ups.

—Robert Brault

❖ ❖ ❖

I don't care how poor a man is; if he has family, he's rich.

—Dan Wilcox and Thad Mumford

❖ ❖ ❖

Rejoice with your family in the beautiful land of life!

—Albert Einstein

❖ ❖ ❖

Trust is the glue of life. It's the most essential ingredient in effective communication. It's the foundational principle that holds all relationships.

—Stephen Covey

❖ ❖ ❖

Nothing is perfect. Life is messy. Relationships are complex. Outcomes are uncertain. People are irrational.

—Hugh Mackay

❖ ❖ ❖

My belief is that communication is the best way to create strong relationships.

—Jada Pinkett Smith

❖ ❖ ❖

You can have meaning, accomplishment, engagement and good relationships, even if you are dull on the positive affect side.

—Martin Seligman

❖ ❖ ❖

In good relationships, we are happy to grow as the other person becomes part of us and who we are.

—Miroslav Volf

❖ ❖ ❖

Aggression is inherently destructive of relationships. People and ideologies are pitted against each other, believing that in order to survive, they must destroy the opposition.

—Margaret J. Wheatley

❖ ❖ ❖

The business of business is relationships; the business of life is human connection.

—Robin S. Sharma

❖ ❖ ❖

I think we learn the most from imperfect relationships – things like forgiveness and compassion.

—Andrea Thompson

❖ ❖ ❖

I have very high standards for every part of life – my work, my relationships, food, love. I can't just pretend.

—Olivia Wilde

❖ ❖ ❖

Treasure your relationships, not your possessions.

—Anthony J. D'Angelo

❖ ❖ ❖

Relationships are important, but stay focused on all the things that are important. Figure out what you want.

—Daren Kagasoff

❖ ❖ ❖

Part of growing up is realizing you learn to love so many people. It's about forming those relationships and finding what will last forever.

—Dylan O'Brien

❖ ❖ ❖

All relationships change the brain – but most important are the intimate bonds that foster or fail us, altering the delicate circuits that shape memories, emotions and that ultimate souvenir, the self.

—Diane Ackerman

❖ ❖ ❖

Distance is a bad excuse for not having a good relationship with somebody. It's the determination to keep it going or let it fall by the wayside; that's the real reason that the relationships continue.

—James McAvoy

❖ ❖ ❖

Our business is about technology, yes. But it's also about operations and customer relationships.

—Michael Dell

❖ ❖ ❖

Everyone desires relationships and community. Most people want to belong to a cohesive, like-minded group. It staves off loneliness. It promotes identity. These are natural and very human instincts.

—Joshua Ferris

❖ ❖ ❖

At the end of the day I have always seen the end of my relationships as a personal failure. There is nothing ever pretty in saying goodbye.

—Elisabetta Canalis

❖ ❖ ❖

When you acknowledge the integrity of your solitude, and settle into its mystery, your relationships with others take on a new warmth, adventure and wonder.

—John O'Donohue

❖ ❖ ❖

Business is not just doing deals; business is having great products, doing great engineering, and providing tremendous service to customers. Finally, business is a cobweb of human relationships.

—Ross Perot

❖ ❖ ❖

I take inspiration from everything around me, also relationships and friends. And the inside of my crazy head.

—Ellie Goulding

❖ ❖ ❖

The single most important factor in our long-term happiness is the relationships we have with our family and close friends.

—Clayton Christensen

❖ ❖ ❖

I work more now because at this time of my life I am not disturbed from my aim by outside pressures such as family, passionate relationships, dealing with 'who am I?' – those complications when one is searching for one's self.

—Jeanne Moreau

❖ ❖ ❖

Religion creates community, community creates altruism and altruism turns us away from self and towards the common good... There is something about the tenor of relationships within a religious community that makes it the best tutorial in citizenship and good neighborliness.

—Jonathan Sacks

❖ ❖ ❖

Wealth is the progressive realization of worthy goals, the ability to love and have compassion, meaningful and caring relationships.

—Deepak Chopra

❖ ❖ ❖

Pride adversely affects all our relationships – our relationship with God and His servants, between husband and wife, parent and child, employer and employee, teacher and student, and all mankind.

—Ezra Taft Benson

❖ ❖ ❖

Things happen to everybody in the course of a lifetime. Relationships end, people die, tragedy befalls everyone. So everyone has this wealth of experience, and the older you are the more you have to draw on.

—Eric Stoltz

❖ ❖ ❖

As you learn who you are, you can better surround yourself with friends who make you a better person, and that sometimes only happens when you disassemble old relationships.

—Maggie Stiefvater

❖ ❖ ❖

Men and women do think differently, and frankly, we don't understand each other. Not at all! But that's what makes relationships so amazing.

—Kevin Hart

❖ ❖ ❖

I have very little faith that I'll ever find someone. I've had some bad luck and I've made some bad choices – not in men, but in how I've chosen to deal with relationships.

—**Selma Blair**

❖ ❖ ❖

I think relationships are really hard. Each one gives you lessons that you need.

—**Jennifer Grey**

❖ ❖ ❖

PROFESSION

Teaching is a very noble profession that shapes the character, caliber, and future of an individual. If the people remember me as a good teacher, that will be the biggest honour for me.

—A.P.J. Abdul Kalam

❖ ❖ ❖

To become an able and successful man in any profession, three things are necessary, nature, study and practice.

—Henry Ward Beecher

❖ ❖ ❖

Every person who has mastered a profession is a skeptic concerning it.

—George Bernard Shaw

❖ ❖ ❖

Never call an accountant a credit to his profession; a good accountant is a debit to his profession.

—Charles Lyell

❖ ❖ ❖

I'm lucky to be in a profession where you can keep getting better.

—Cy Coleman

❖ ❖ ❖

Professionalism is not sportsmanship. If you don't succeed, you won't be in your profession for long. In our society, it's not about good or bad. It's about who's on top.

—Chili Davis

❖ ❖ ❖

The courage of a soldier is heightened by his knowledge of his profession.

—Publius Flavius Vegetius Renatus

❖ ❖ ❖

Frustrations are going to be there in every profession you're in.

—Raphael Saadiq

❖ ❖ ❖

It does not matter how slowly you go as long as you do not stop.

—Confucius

❖ ❖ ❖

I Never dreamed about success I worked for it.

—Estee Lauder

❖ ❖ ❖

The best way to find yourself is to lose yourself in the service of others.

—Gandhi

❖ ❖ ❖

Treat your customers like they own you. Because they do.

—Mark Cuban

❖ ❖ ❖

Professional is not a label you give yourself – it's a description you have others will apply to you.

—David Maister

❖ ❖ ❖

Nothing is particularly hard if you divided into small jobs.

—Henry Ford

Leaders don't make excuse. They create result.

—Robin Sharma

❖ ❖ ❖

WORK ETHICS

What you do is what matters, not what you think or say or plan.

—Jason Fried

❖ ❖ ❖

If you work hard enough and assert yourself, and use your mind and imagination, you can shape the world to your desires.

—Malcolm Gladwell

❖ ❖ ❖

Plan your work for today and every day, then work your plan.

—Margaret Thatcher

❖ ❖ ❖

Who you are tomorrow begins with what you do today.

—Tim Fargo

❖ ❖ ❖

The harder I work, the luckier I get.

—Samuel Goldwyn

❖ ❖ ❖

It's not what you do but that kind of job you do that makes the difference.

—Ben Carson

❖ ❖ ❖

Talent is cheaper than table salt. What separates the talented individual from the successful one is a lot of hard work.

—Stephen King

❖ ❖ ❖

Are great things ever done smoothly? Time, patience, and indomitable will must show. Great work requires great and persistent effort for a long time. Character has to be established through a thousand stumbles.

—Swami Vivekananda

❖ ❖ ❖

It's hard to beat a person who never gives up.

—Babe Ruth

❖ ❖ ❖

The difference between try and triumph is just a little umph!

—Marvin Phillips

❖ ❖ ❖

I learned the value of hard work by working hard.

—Margaret Mead

❖ ❖ ❖

Always make a total effort, even when the odds are against you.

—Arnold Palmer

❖ ❖ ❖

Nothing worth having comes easy.

—Theodore Roosevelt

❖ ❖ ❖

Nobody ever drowned in his own sweat.

—Ann Landers

❖ ❖ ❖

In the middle of difficulty lies opportunity.

—Albert Einstein

❖ ❖ ❖

I'm a greater believer in luck, and I find the harder I work the more I have of it.

—Thomas Jefferson

❖ ❖ ❖

All roads that lead to success have to pass through hard work boulevard at some point.

—Eric Thomas

❖ ❖ ❖

Satisfaction lies in the effort, not in the attainment. Full effort is full victory.

—Mohandas Gandhi

❖ ❖ ❖

The difference between the impossible and the possible lies in a person's determination.

—Tommy Lasorda

❖ ❖ ❖

No shortcuts, work for it.

—Unknown

❖ ❖ ❖

Working hard and working smart sometimes can be two different things.

—Byron Dorgan

❖ ❖ ❖

Working hard is great, being lazy sometimes is great, but failed potential is the worst.

—Campbell Scott

❖ ❖ ❖

By doing well the duty, which is nearest to us, the duty which is in our hands now, we make ourselves stronger; and improving our strength in this manner step by step, we may reach a state in which it shall be our privilege to do the most coveted and honoured duties in life and in society.

—Swami Vivekananda

❖ ❖ ❖

The world belongs to the energetic.

—Ralph Waldo Emerson

❖ ❖ ❖

The first and the best victory is to conquer self.

—Plato

❖ ❖ ❖

The only way to do great work is to love what you do.

—Steve Jobs

❖ ❖ ❖

There are no shortcuts to any place worth going.

—Beverly Sills

❖ ❖ ❖

WEALTH

Don't gain the world & lose your soul, wisdom is better than silver or gold.

—Bob Marley

❖ ❖ ❖

Wealth consists not in having great possessions, but in having few wants.

—Epictetus

❖ ❖ ❖

Seek not greater wealth, but simpler pleasure; not higher fortune, but deeper felicity.

—Mahatma Gandhi

❖ ❖ ❖

Wealth is the ability to fully experience life.

—Henry David Thoreau

❖ ❖ ❖

It is health that is real wealth and not pieces of gold and silver.

—Mahatma Gandhi

❖ ❖ ❖

Wealth is like sea-water; the more we drink, the thirstier we become; and the same is true of fame.

—Arthur Schopenhauer

❖ ❖ ❖

If a man is proud of his wealth, he should not be praised until it is known how he employs it.

—Socrates

❖ ❖ ❖

Wealth is the product of man's capacity to think.

—Ayn Rand

❖ ❖ ❖

Wealth stays with us a little moment if at all: only our characters are steadfast, not our gold.

—Euripides

❖ ❖ ❖

We have no more right to consume happiness without producing it than to consume wealth without producing it.

—George Bernard Shaw

❖ ❖ ❖

Power and wealth are not two of my main stakes.

—Ratan Tata

❖ ❖ ❖

Contentment is the only real wealth.

—Alfred Nobel

❖ ❖ ❖

It is great wealth to a soul to live frugally with a contented mind.

—Lucretius

❖ ❖ ❖

It is not the creation of wealth that is wrong, but the love of money for its own sake.

—Margaret Thatcher

❖ ❖ ❖

We'll never solve the feminization of power until we solve the masculinity of wealth.

—Gloria Steinem

❖ ❖ ❖

Wars are caused by undefended wealth.

—Ernest Hemingway

❖ ❖ ❖

The wealth of information now available at the click of a finger amazes me.

—A.P.J. Abdul Kalam

❖ ❖ ❖

I have no riches but my thoughts. Yet these are wealth enough for me.

—Sara Teasdale

❖ ❖ ❖

Where there are friends there is wealth.

—Plautus

❖ ❖ ❖

Wealth is not his that has it, but his that enjoys it.

—Benjamin Franklin

❖ ❖ ❖

Wealthy people have not disappeared, they are just not so willing to show off their wealth.

—Martin Parr

❖ ❖ ❖

The only wealth which you will keep forever is the wealth you have given away.

—Marcus Aurelius

❖ ❖ ❖

Neither wealth or greatness render us happy.

—Jean de La Fontaine

❖ ❖ ❖

Fear of death increases in exact proportion to increase in wealth.

—Ernest Hemingway

❖ ❖ ❖

When Honor's sun declines, and Wealth takes wings, Then Learning shines, the best of precious things.

—Edward Cocker

❖ ❖ ❖

I had one idea that never changed in my mind – that you should use your wealth to help people.

—Chuck Feeney

❖ ❖ ❖

BUSINESS NETWORKING

My Golden Rule of Networking is simple: Don't keep score.

—Harvey Mackay

❖ ❖ ❖

Succeeding in Business is all about Making Connection.

—Richard Branson

❖ ❖ ❖

The Opposite of Networking is: Not Working.

—Unknown

❖ ❖ ❖

Networking means the act exchanging information with people who can help you professionally.

—Michele Jenne

❖ ❖ ❖

Everyone should build their networking before they need it.

—Dave Delaney

❖ ❖ ❖

The richest people in the world look for and build networks, everyone else looks for work.

—Robert Kiyosaki

❖ ❖ ❖

It occurs to me that our survival may depend upon our talking to one another.

—Dan Simmons, Hyperion

❖ ❖ ❖

When you invite people to share in your miracle, you create future allies during rough weather.

—Shannon L. Alder

❖ ❖ ❖

Leaders empower individuals by building trust and coaching competence in their job roles and networking skills.

—Kenneth H. Blanchard

❖ ❖ ❖

Two people that have the same wants are two people that should be friends.

—Shannon L. Alder

❖ ❖ ❖

One of the main reasons people are not rich is that they worry too much about things that might never happen.

—Robert Kiyosaki Glinda Harris

❖ ❖ ❖

If your business is not on the internet, then your business will be out of business.

—Bill Gates

❖ ❖ ❖

If you become teachable and remain so, a network marketing career will make you money. More importantly it will mold your character.

—Jay Vandenhoff

❖ ❖ ❖

Success is the ability to go from one failure to another with no loss of enthusiasm.

—Sir Winston Churchill

❖ ❖ ❖

Networking is an essential part of building wealth.

—Armstrong Williams

❖ ❖ ❖

Build a relationship with people you do serious business, One can escape a deal but not a relations easily.

—SunitaBiddhu

❖ ❖ ❖